SIX
SECULAR
PHILOSOPHERS

SIX
SECULAR
PHILOSOPHERS

Lewis White Beck

*Professor of Philosophy in
the University of Rochester*

THE FREE PRESS, *New York*

COLLIER-MACMILLAN LIMITED, *London*

CONTENTS

Preface 7

I What Is Secular Philosophy? 9

II Families of Secular Philosophers 18

III Spinoza 27

IV Hume 42

V Kant 61

VI Nietzsche 79

VII James 92

VIII Santayana 106

Notes 119

Index 125

To Charles Mills

PREFACE

Although the philosophers studied in this book contributed much to present-day secularism, they contributed even more to the conception of liberal religion. Modernism is not a peculiarly modern movement. Its beginnings were earlier than Darwinism, psychoanalysis, and the Social Gospel, and are to be found in the writings of philosophers in the main stream of European thought. Their critical estimation of religion—leading sometimes to its rejection, sometimes to efforts at its reform—is important to all those who are troubled over the position and function of religion in our culture and in a divided world. In this book I have discussed six philosophers whose works on religion seem to me to be most germane to contemporary issues: Spinoza, Hume, Kant, Nietzsche, James, and Santayana.

In the winter of 1958-1959 I gave a series of lectures on these thinkers to The Brick Forum of The Brick Presbyterian Church in Rochester; since then, several of them have been delivered before other groups in the United States and Canada. The vigorous response of my audiences—sympathetic, often critical, always constructive—and many requests for copies of the lectures embolden me to have them published. They are given here almost exactly as they were orally presented; but the questions raised by listeners gave me, here and there, occasion to clarify points that may have been left obscure in their original form.

LEWIS WHITE BECK

March 9, 1960

I

What Is Secular Philosophy?

What is secular philosophy? This is a simple question, but if an answer is not to be overly simple and dogmatic, we must come to it in what may at first appear to be a roundabout way. We must first discuss the meanings of the words "religion," "theology," and "philosophy" before we consider the word "secular."

What, then, is religion? There is a constant danger that when we try to think logically about religion, we may surreptitiously convert it into something strictly intellectual that is easy to analyze, as if it were just a way of thinking that we are examining. Religion does include a set of beliefs about God, and these beliefs are meaningful or meaningless, true or false, and as such they can be examined intellectually. But religion is more than such a set of beliefs. The word also refers to attitudes that people have and act upon when they do believe that God exists. The word also refers to conduct following upon these attitudes, not just to the beliefs that are held about God and man and their relationship.

There are so many different conceptions of God that what one man considers his religious beliefs and attitudes may seem to someone else to be the most arrant atheism; a wit in France in the eighteenth century referred to someone as an atheist "because he believes in only one god." To be quite neutral and fair, I suppose we shall have to say that if anyone sincerely professes to believe in God, then whatever attitudes are associated with this belief and whatever practices flow from it constitute his religion. There are "private religions" which meet this definition; but when the belief and attitude are shared, and the resulting conduct, rituals, and practices are given an institutional form, we have the meaning of "religion" as ordinarily used. We will not mean by religion anything so broad that we should have to say, for instance, that communism and capitalism are opposing "religions," or anything so narrow that we could exclude established sects with which we happen not to be sympathetic.

When we speak of religion in this way, we put the emphasis upon action which is based upon belief *in* God. Believing *in* something is not quite the same thing as believing *that* this something exists. The latter is merely a substitute for knowing that it exists; "I believe I have some money in my pocket" is a poor substitute for "I know I have some money in my pocket." But neither believing nor knowing that I have entails any particular attitude towards it; I can believe that something is the case and be uninterested or approving or disapproving. Believing *in* something, however, is an active faith in and commitment to what is believed; it cannot be separated from our attitudes and emotions, for it depends upon them as well as upon our opinions or knowledge of the thing.

Believing *in* God is religious act; believing *that* God exists is a theoretical or cognitive act that does not necessarily indicate that the person who has this belief is religious in his attitude or action. But for every belief *in* something, there is a corresponding belief *that* something is the case; one does not believe *in* God unless he believes *that* God exists. Still, the two kinds of belief, even when directed to the same thing, are psychologically quite different.

Theology is the systematic organization of beliefs *that* God exists and of beliefs about God, in the theoretical sense

of belief. Theology is, or claims to be, a division of knowledge. It is theory about God. The fundamental principles
of theology may be taken from Scripture, from revelation,
from pure reason, from our understanding of nature; so we
have corresponding kinds of theology (biblical theology, revealed theology, rational theology, and natural theology).
Each set of religious beliefs in God has a corresponding set
of beliefs about God, so there is a Mohammedan theology
and a Christian theology, a Catholic theology and a Protestant theology, and the like. All of them are elaborations of the
beliefs about the God that some religious people believe in.

When one asks, "What is philosophy, and what is its relation to theology and religion?" the only proper response is
to ask another question, namely, "Whose theology, whose
religion, and whose philosophy are you inquiring about?"
Philosophies, religions, and theologies have varied so much
over the centuries and exist in such variety today that no
single simple answer can be given to questions about their
relationship. If one says, "Philosophy is related to religion in
such and such a way," he means or he ought to mean that a
particular set of philosophical doctrines—usually the one he
accepts—is related in a specific way to a particular set of
theological beliefs and religious practices—a set which he may
himself accept or reject.

The variety of possible relations between philosophies and
theologies may be illustrated by three different views which
have been widely accepted in the history of Christianity.

In the Middle Ages, philosophy was regarded as the handmaiden to theology. Theological truths were revealed to man
and had become fixed and established in the Church. The
task of the philosopher was not to challenge these beliefs, but
to prepare the mind for accepting them by answering criti-
cisms of them and by giving them the dress of reason. For
instance, it was believed that the existence of God was a
revealed truth; but not all men acknowledged the validity
of this revelation. The task of the philosopher was, accord-

ingly, to give proofs of the existence of God, not by appealing to revelation, but by appealing only to truths of reason
and nature, which were known even to those who rejected
faith and revelation. Faith, to be sure, went beyond what
could be proved in this way, and it was a sure path of certainty for men who were not sufficiently reasonable or sufficiently well educated to follow the proofs found, for instance,
in the works of St. Thomas Aquinas. But reason could go a
long way unaided by revelation; it was a preamble to and an
elaboration of the subtleties of faith, not its rival or a substitute.

This conception of the role of the philosopher is still held
in the Catholic Church.[1] In this conception the philosopher
is intellectually free to think what he will so long as his
conclusions are either irrelevant to the revealed teaching of
the church or in conformity to it, and he has a positive duty
to use his intellect for the elaboration and defense of its
teaching. But when his conclusions conflict with this higher
truth, they are not only heretical but also false. For theology
is held to be definite knowledge vouchsafed to man and to
be superior to philosophy, which is only the highest form of
human knowledge, i.e., of knowledge gained by the use of
men's rational talents unaided by revelation. This, then, is
one answer to the question of the relation between philosophy
and religion and theology.

A very different view of the relation was held in the so-
called Age of Reason. This period in the history of the European mind followed the Renaissance and the Reformation.
Men became tired of the endless debates of theologians,
disillusioned with the certitude they claimed and proclaimed
in the name of faith, sickened by the tortures and wars which
arose from the head-on clash of incompatible dogmas. They
now asserted the right to think their own thoughts and to
defend them publicly, and to reject the authoritarian teach-
ing-office of the Church. The handmaiden to theology, like

many other servants, turned on her former mistress, and regarded herself as superior to the menial work assigned to her in earlier times. Philosophy claimed autonomy. However much this may have appeared at the time as rank heresy and irreligion, it did not immediately lead to much of what we would now call antireligious thought or activity. The climate of opinion was not one in which men were ready to abandon the truths of theology in which they had been nurtured; most of the thinkers of the time were not yet ready to conclude that religion as a whole was antirational.

But the times called for philosophers who could support the venerable doctrines of theology with better arguments and with fewer appeals to dubious supernatural revelation, which, when not validated by reason, easily sinks into superstition. Reason became first the judge of revelation, and John Locke wrote, "He that takes away reason to make way for revelation puts out the light of both"; soon reason came to be a substitute for it. Thus in the seventeenth and eighteenth centuries there was a persistent attempt to save religion from revealed theology and its obscurantism; there were many books with such typical titles as *The Reasonableness of Christianity, Christianity Not Mysterious,* and *Christianity as Old as the Creation.* In the period when both political and religious tolerance was growing, efforts were made to find basic theological principles so reasonable that no one could fail to be convinced of them. Spinoza formulated ultimate principles for a universal religion, and Leibniz, one of the greatest philosophers of the age, spent many years in a futile effort to bring Catholics and Protestants together by minimizing their differences and magnifying their agreements in the common ground of reason as cultivated in his philosophy.

Let us skip another two centuries and come to the present to find another theory of the relation of philosophy to theology and religion. There are innumerable philosophies and religions today, and I cannot venture to describe any of them as typical of our century, as the "religion of reason" was typical of both the theology and the philosophy of the Age of Reason. But I shall take one prominent movement in recent philosophy, the school of philosophy known as Positivism. According to nineteenth century positivists such as Auguste Comte, religion represents a stage in the history of the mind from which we are gradually emerging. Truths that men can really discover are not the truths about the gods and the human soul, but truths about nature; and the way to their discovery is science. The task of the philosopher, as seen by the positivists, was to extend the success of the historic rôle of science by concentrating human talents upon solvable problems, instead of allowing us to continue to waste our efforts on the unsolvable problems of metaphysics and theology. Not being willing to give up the moral fervor of religion, however, Comte proposed and attempted to establish a "religion of humanity," a religion without a theology, in which great thinkers and scientists and contributors to human well-being would be honored as the saints.

More recent positivists base their teaching more upon a study of language and logic than upon the history of thought, but with respect to religion they come to similar conclusions, though without the quixotism of the "religion of humanity." They say that statements that cannot be verified by methods that are in principle like those of the scientist are pseudo-statements; they are neither provable nor refutable; they are nonsense. Statements of theologians such as "God exists" look like statements scientists make, such as "Atoms exist," but in fact they are quite different. The theologians' statements cannot be tested to find out whether they are true or false, and hence we cannot ascribe any definite cognitive meaning to them. They may give some emotional satisfaction to those who believe them, but they have no determinable objective meaning, and the satisfaction they give is only emotional and perhaps spurious. The task of the philosopher is to clean out the Augean stables of metaphysical, ethical, and theological nonsense so that we can get on with the work proper to our intellect, which is the understanding, anticipation, and control of nature—a work that has been inhibited in the past by beliefs in "higher things" that at best degraded the scientific study of "mere fact" and at worst denied its results. Philosophy, like psychoanalysis, is a therapeutic device to keep us from being misled by symbols which express only our own wishes and needs and fears, but which seem to indicate an obscure and important kind of objective fact.

These three examples, I hope, suffice to show that we cannot say that there is any single simple relation between philosophy and religion. It all depends upon the kind of philosophy and the kind of religion we are talking about. I began, in my first example, by describing a philosophy oriented around and governed by religion; my second and third were examples of secular philosophy.

The word "secular" refers to the world considered in contradistinction to the Church. The dictionary defines it as meaning "not bound by monastic vows or rules." Among religious people, it is now often used as a term of abuse. Secular philosophy means philosophy which is autonomous with respect to established and accepted religious views. It is not one which is, as medieval philosophy was, tacitly or openly committed to drawing conclusions authorized in advance by religion and guaranteed by ecclesiastical authority to be true. Secular philosophy is not necessarily antireligious;[2] its conclusions are not necessarily opposed to religious beliefs. But if the conclusions of a secular philosopher do diverge from the beliefs of religion, he will not say, "*Mea culpa!* I must have made a mistake." He will say, rather, "So much the worse for those who have not thought this through, and who have accepted on faith something that my philosophical examination shows to be false."

Rarely is a philosopher's thought completely free from the

beliefs in which he was brought up. A philosopher shows marks of the intellectual climate in which he lives, and often shares in the religious beliefs and puzzles of his contemporaries. His secularism is a matter of degree, not something simply present or absent. Those who conscientiously try to be independent in their thinking sometimes have to admit that their thinking is not as free as they hoped to make it. If they themselves do not recognize this, their biographers surely will point out how much influence their religious environment had upon their thought, even when their views were explicitly hostile to the religion.

However secular a philosopher may be—indeed, however hostile he may become to religion—there remains a deep and integral connection between what concerns him as a philosopher and what the religious person believes and does. Philosophy is not so much a particular and exclusive set of beliefs different from those of other fields of knowledge as it is an attitude of mind and a discipline towards fundamental questions wherever they emerge. The subject matter of philosophy is, or aims to be, the whole of human experience. Philosophy thus has direct contact with science, morals, history, art, politics, and religion. In so far as religious beliefs are beliefs about the linkage that a religious person feels between himself and what he regards as the ultimate reality and the source of his being and destiny, the subject matter of religious thought and that of philosophy overlap at least in part.

No one can survey the whole of experience; each philosopher takes some part of it with which he is familiar and of whose importance he is convinced. He then reads the rest of experience in the terms of that portion. In the history of all civilizations, religion has been one of the key experiences which philosophers have used again and again to open what they think are the gates to wisdom. So long as the religious experience was the only one which counted for much among contemplative people, as in the Middle Ages, the division between philosophy and theology was hard to draw; most of the great philosophers were also great theologians, even if they recognized a dividing line between their two offices. Philosophy and theology had the same kind of problems, and they had to come up with some of the same answers.

Today, experiences other than religious ones are generally believed to be more significant for philosophy; we live in a "secural age," and the philosopher more often appears as a critic of theology than as its handmaiden. But even now a man is hardly likely to be considered a philosopher unless he has some well-reasoned views on some of the matters that lie within the traditional scope of theology, even if his view be that theological opinions about such matters are false or nonsensical. If the theologian and philosopher were not concerned with some of the same problems—problems we might collect together under the vague name of questions about the "meaning of things"—they would ignore each other, as the scientist and theologian have learned to do by cutting the world up into two parts and assigning a share to each.

If the philosopher and theologian did this, however, not just for the purpose of the solution of some of the intricate problems of the one or the other but as a genuine divorce between their concerns, the loss to each would be irreparable. The religious consciousness not continuously scrutinized by reason has an inevitable tendency to degenerate into superstition; and religious practices not continuously examined by free moral judgment have always declined into empty ritualism. On the other hand, the synoptic function of the philosopher, who is supposed to see things steadily and see them whole, is lost if the philosopher does not remain sensitive to those concerns which have given religion its central place in life. Without this sensitivity, philosophers only take in each other's technical washing in logic and epistemology and metaphysics, and do not keep alive that wonder in which, Aristotle said, all philosophy begins.

II

Families of Secular Philosophers

In choosing philosophers to illustrate the secular concern with religious questions, we should be guided by two criteria. First, the philosopher should really be secular in his motives and procedures, and not just a theologian who, like many eminent theologians, happens to have written books of philosophy. I have tried to choose men whose independence of mind was such that they often appeared to their contemporaries to be enemies of religion; two of them, anyway, were at least mildly persecuted by their theological opponents.

Second, they should be philosophers whose scope is so large that they are not secular by default, as it were; they will be philosophers whose interests and concerns were so broad that they could not evade a philosophical scrutiny of religion. We should not choose men who have philosophized on other problems but ignored religious questions, though they would be, of course, secular in a trivial sense of the word. I have chosen only philosophers who philosophized in what might be called "the grand tradition" or who worked on "the perennial problems," whose theories were of such catholicity and profundity that they had a direct bearing upon religious beliefs even when the philosophers were not explicitly discussing theological questions. They are men who investigated matters which the religious person normally takes on faith and without investigation, matters which the religious person sometimes feels it is impious to investigate by cool and critical reason.

Another criterion has been given at least a secondary place: the philosophers chosen should be philosophers whose works are addressed to and understood by the educated layman, not philosophers whose works are so difficult and technical that they can be read only by other philosophers. In our group of six philosophers, we have included four of the best writers in the history of modern philosophy, and only one of them (Kant) can be considered difficult to read in his own words.

The six philosophers chosen are: Spinoza, Hume, Kant, Nietzsche, James, and Santayana. In our group are one Jew, one Catholic, and four Protestants; one Dutchman, one Scotsman, two Germans, and two Americans; one from the seventeenth, two from the eighteenth, and three from the late nineteenth and the twentieth centuries.

There are deeper affiliations among some of them than indicated in this somewhat external classification. In fact, the six philosophers, judged in the light of the kind of problem which was uppermost in their philosophies of religion, belong in two distinct families. In the first family are the philosophers who took science and philosophy as limiting the scope and validity and content of religious belief. In the second are the philosophers who were most concerned with the relation of religious values to the other values in life and culture. The first family consists of Spinoza, Hume, and Kant; the second, of Nietzsche, James, and Santayana. Kant, however, might be considered a rightful member of either group because his way of thinking about religion and his identification of the crucial religious problem is transitional between them; but for chronological reasons it is perhaps better to place him along with Spinoza and Hume.

In the seventeenth and eighteenth centuries every thinker

had to come to terms with science, which seemed at last to be giving real objective knowledge to replace the speculations, revelations, and controversies of the theologians. To meet the impact of epoch-making discoveries in science, like that of the Copernican astronomy in the middle of the sixteenth century, philosophers who were concerned with religion had recourse to one of three general strategies.

The first was to make a religion out of science itself, or, perhaps more accurately, to direct men's religious aspirations away from an unknown supernatural being and toward the world itself, whose physical and mathematical structure was to be made known by science. This strategy sought to attract the best efforts of men, both intellectually and morally, away from that obscure world of mystery which Europe had inherited partly from the Bible and partly from the later Greeks, and to which they had so long directed their major talents that the understanding and control of nature had been delayed for centuries. Some philosophers attempted to preserve the religious fervor and conviction that were challenged by those who painted the vivid scientific picture of the universe as a vast piece of machinery, and they did so by picturing the world-machine itself as a proper object of religious veneration and reverence. This was the strategy of Spinoza.

The second strategy was adopted in the next century by David Hume, after science had scored still more triumphs and the religious ardor of the seventeenth century had become attenuated in the cool reasonableness of the English Enlightenment. Hume said that we cannot simply decide that the God of the traditional religious conception does not exist and then find a substitute for Him in the world disclosed by science, and worship that. This would be cant, for the world revealed by science is neither itself a worthy object of religious reverence nor evidence of another object, above and beyond it, which would satisfy man's religious needs. No, said Hume, let us in honesty leave the content of religious belief what it has ever been (and as unreasonable as Hume judged it to be), and then let us ask: In the light of what we know from science and from what it is reasonable to suppose that we shall discover as science progresses, are the religious beliefs true? His answer was: We do not know them to be certainly true; and if they are probably true, this probability is not great enough to warrant efforts to reform ourselves or society by reference to them. Indeed, Hume goes further: he is not convinced that such a reform is even desirable, and he invidiously compares traditional religious morals with the morals of common sense enlightened by a knowledge of human nature and history.

The third strategy was to accept Hume's premise and one of his conclusions, but to deny the other conclusion. Kant agreed with Hume that the traditional view of religious truth was unreasonable, and that no religious belief can be confirmed by the scientific interpretation of nature. If we demand theoretical knowledge as a basis for religion, Hume and Kant were at one in saying that there was no ground for religion. But where Hume had concluded, "So much the worse for religion," Kant said that there was another basis for religion which was just as reasonable as the one he and Hume had rejected. This was our moral consciousness. True religion could be built upon the data of morality and a rational examination of the moral consciousness, just as Spinoza had thought it could be based upon the data of theoretical philosophy and science. But, of course, the edifice of religion would be changed to make it fit the new foundation.

With Kant there was a clear separation of the scope of science from that of religion. Science and religion were not, for him, allies, as they had been for Spinoza, nor were they enemies and rivals, as Hume had seen them to be. For Kant, they expressed different attitudes and they had different ob-

jects and purposes. Kant's theory has sometimes been called
a "two-world theory" because of the sharp separation he
made between the realms of knowledge and of faith, between
the world of nature, which we can know scientifically, and
a supernatural world, which we cannot know, between the
world of fact and the realm of value.

Between the death of Kant in 1804 and that of Nietzsche
in 1900, the center of religious controversy, at least between
advanced thinkers in both theology and philosophy, shifted
to a quite different position from that around which debate
in the seventeenth and eighteenth centuries had turned. It
moved in the direction pointed out in Kant's philosophy: towards exploiting the divergent implications of the diverse
commitments to factual inquiry and the pursuit of values.
The fundamental motives of the shift after the middle of
the century, however, lay not so much in the widespread influence of Kant's own philosophy as in the reverberations of
the most important intellectual event in the nineteenth century, the publication of *The Origin of Species* in 1859. It is
given to few works in any science to have the revolutionary
effect Darwin's book had, and its immediate effect was to
reopen, for a short and stormy period, the old warfare between the biblical and the scientific interpretations of man's
early history. This conflict between Genesis and the theory of
evolution lasts to this day in many circles; but among thinking people in both camps the victory of Darwinism as an
interpretation of man's origin was so complete that by the
end of the century the Kantian treaty of peace was again
almost in full force. The autonomies of science and philosophy were so well established that, though they had to be
defended from time to time, most of the attacks on them
came from the ignorant instead of from the learned. Religious claims for hegemony in the field of science had been
struck down so violently that the Kantian refuge, adjusted
and reorganized in various ways, was taken by many theo-

logians; within this refuge, they could be satisfied that no serious religious doctrine, properly defended, need be considered in jeopardy from science. They then gave up the burden of trying to regard the Bible as a scientific textbook and religion as a competitor of science in the understanding of nature. The battle fought by Spinoza, Hume, and Kant had been won; science and theology came to a *modus vivendi* of peaceful coexistence. Though some echoes of the old battle can be heard in the works of Nietzsche, James, and Santayana, these men's hearts were not in this battle, and the chief controversies over religion were not fought out along the old lines at all.

The new line itself goes back to Kant, with his doctrine that the truth and validity of religion is based upon men's ethical concerns and not upon their understanding of nature or their claims to metaphysical knowledge. The question is: How and to what extent is religion to be justified in a world in which answers to questions of fact and to many if not all questions about the management of human affairs are to be found by continuing the march of science into ever-new fields? Do men—even the ignorant masses of men to whom many sophisticated critics of religion had recommended it as an opiate—need religion in a time when the extension of scientific discipline is required if science is to fulfill its promise of increasing knowledge without end and of extending man's domination over nature? That was the question, and perhaps the most typical answers of the early part of our century were either, on the one hand, atheism and materialism and secularism and scientism—taking all these words in their more pejorative sense—or, on the other, some vague kind of humanism, of religion as a muscularly optimistic life-affirmation without any theological underpinnings.

The three recent philosophers selected by our criteria did not make this easy choice and facile affirmation. They were all first-rate philosophers, not propagandists for a jejune and undemanding faith. None of them was a Kantian in the technical philosophical sense of the term, but each was like Kant in his recognition of the seriousness and difficulty of the issue; and at least two of them and perhaps all three were almost Kantian in the solidity and profundity of their commitment to an intellectual understanding of moral concerns. In each of them we find an earnest struggling with the problem of the status of fundamental human values which had been the traditional concern of religion, values which seemed to become precarious and rootless with the general decline of the religious consciousness. Hence their philosophies escape some of the insipid and superficial optimism of those who would have said, had they not believed it was already too late, "*Écrasons l'infâme!*"

Nietzsche gave a negative answer to the question of whether religion can be justified by reference to values. He saw religious illusion as one of the heaviest fetters to be thrown off if men are to come to their full estate and to be masters of their destiny; it had fulfilled its function of taming and disciplining men—indeed, it had fulfilled this function all to well, Nietzsche thought; but the time had come to throw off its restraints in favor of those values of life which it had denigrated and denied.

James and Santayana saw an error in Nietzsche's making what is actual (as Nietzsche saw it: the fact that all actions spring from a natural will to power) the standard of what ought to be. James saw human vision of what ought to be made real as a dynamic factor necessary for human well-being and dignity, and he defended the belief in whatever is necessary for this dynamism of human aspiration to be historically and morally effective. He thus favored a religious hypothesis as one's own venture, perhaps as one's own venture against the world and certainly as one's own venture against a conservative and unadventuresome church; he thus recommended a religious attitude and a belief in God or some gods with little regard to the established forms or traditions of religion or to the facts of well-established sciences.

Santayana, finally, thought of religion in a much less activistic form than James and Nietzsche did. To him, religion was a myth to be taken seriously but not literally. Taken literally, it conflicted with fact and could not be defended. Taken figuratively, for its meaning in terms of human values, it was a necessary part of the life of spirit and culture. It was one form of the pursuit of values, a form that he thought had been interpreted in too restricted a way by Kant, Nietzsche, and James. "Religion," he writes, "is not to be condemned as a poor substitute for something better, but as a moral consolation and relief from a situation which, but for its presence, would have been infinitely worse."[1]

Another way of looking at our six philosophers would put them in quite a different arrangement, with new oppositions and affiliations among them. This would be to judge them according to the outcome of their thinking, not according to the specific kind of problem that engaged them.

Looked at in this way, we should find a line connecting Spinoza, Hume, and Nietzsche as primarily critics, negative critics, of religion as ordinarily understood. We should find, in moving down this line, a progressive emasculation of theology and denial of the truth and value of religion, a transition from the cold *deus sive natura* of Spinoza to the "God is dead" of Nietzsche, with Hume's agnosticism and ironic recommendation of faith in the middle.

In the second group we should find a progressive rejuvenation of faith in the values of religion, once the literal truth and theoretical certainty of theology had been shown by criticism to be empty and invalid. In Kant, and again in Santayana, there is religion simply as a way of interpreting morality and giving a vivid form to our experience of values, with James close to Kant in his emphasis upon the pragmatic justification of an "over-belief" that is supposed to give a metaphysical support to our emotional and moral concerns.

Since the first organization of these philosophers into families corresponds to their chronological order, however, we shall, by following that order, be dealing together with philosophers who dealt with the same problems. But this other kinship should not be overlooked.

With these introductions to the members of the family of secular philosophers, let us now turn to their lives and words. In what follows, I shall try to be the spokesman, in turn, for each of the philosophers. I shall report or repeat what they said. The reader will decide who among them, if any, is correct.

Suggested Readings

Beck, Lewis White. *Philosophic Inquiry, an Introduction to Philosophy* (Chap. 9). New York: Prentice-Hall, 1952.

Burtt, Edwin Arthur. *Types of Religious Philosophy.* New York: Harper & Brothers, 2nd ed., 1951.

Kaufmann, Walter. A *Critique of Philosophy and Religion.* New York: Harper & Brothers, 1958.

III

Spinoza

Few men in the history of philosophy have
been judged in more widely different ways than Spinoza. In
the eighteenth century he was called an atheist, and to say
of a system of philosophy that it was Spinozistic was sufficient to condemn it; even Hume called Spinozism "a hideous
hypothesis." But Novalis called him "the God-intoxicated
Jew," and Heine said, "It is certain that the life of Spinoza
was faultness, pure and unstained as that of his divine cousin
Jesus Christ."

Perhaps in each of these extreme views there is some truth,
but there is also obvious exaggeration. If an atheist is a person who denies that there is a personal God, then Spinoza
was certainly an atheist. But if one grants Spinoza's own
conception of God, one finds in him a single-minded reverence for God that might warrant Novalis' judgment. Certainly Heine's statement is hyperbole, though Spinoza was
in every sense a good and perhaps a saintly man. The truth
about Spinoza, however, is not of the kind that can be summarized in an apothegm or made memorable in an epigram.

Baruch Spinoza was born in Amsterdam in 1632. His
family had emigrated toward the end of the preceding century from Portugal in order to escape from religious persecution there. They and many of their fellows had prospered and
had become substantial citizens in what was then the freest
and one of the most prosperous cities in Europe. They were
allowed to practice their religion without hindrance, and in

the social and economic life of the city they were not imposed upon and held back as they would have been in most other places.

This very acceptance, however, had some untoward consequences. In their prosperity they perhaps felt their vulnerability more keenly than if they had not been so fortunate. The Jewish community felt that it was a guest of the Christian majority and that it should not spawn religious scandals and ideas that the majority would find seditious. They learned a bad lesson from their earlier oppressors and began an inquisition of their own.

It was in this atmosphere that Spinoza, at the age of twenty-four and already known as a brilliant and promising scholar, was brought before the Synagogue on a charge of heresy. It was charged—and in the light of what we know of his later teachings, no doubt correctly charged—that he asserted that the world was God's body, that angels did not exist, that the soul was not separable from the body, and that the Old Testament did not teach the immortality of the soul. Efforts were made to persuade him to recant or at least to agree not to spread these teachings, and when these failed, he was formally excommunicated.

To the extent that outward circumstances and events give a turn to a man's mind, we can ascribe to this excommunication something of the ethical orientation of Spinoza's philosophizing. Philosophy was not for him a purely or merely intellectual pursuit, but a way of life developed and religiously followed when the normal religious and ethical life of a scholarly Jew was suddenly denied to him. Seeing his ambitions, which were in any case modest, thwarted by these circumstances, Spinoza searched for a higher good that would not be contingent upon fortune and the opinions of his fellows. In an early unfinished fragment entitled *On the Improvement of the Understanding*, written in circumstances in which many a young man would have expressed only bitterness, we can see Spinoza looking for a path to something better than anything to be found on the one from which he had been forced. Its opening sentence is:

After experience had taught me that all the usual surroundings of life are vain and futile, seeing that none of the objects of my fears contained anything either good or bad, except in so far as the mind is affected by them, I finally resolved to inquire whether there might not be some real good having the power to communicate itself, which would affect the mind singly to the exclusion of all else; whether, in fact, there might be anything of which the discovery and attainment would enable to me enjoy continuous, supreme, and unending happiness.[1]

It is to this search that we owe Spinoza's unique philosophy. But although the personal poignancy of this passage is unmistakable, in actual fact Spinoza does not seem to have suffered a great deal from the condemnation and ostracism ordered in the sentence of excommunication. Though it was a blow to his natural desire to be accepted by his fellows in the Jewish community, certainly his religious convictions at this time did not make him believe he was actually under any divine sanction or threat of divine punishment. The image of Spinoza as a melancholy outcast is certainly erroneous, though no one could regard his position at this time as an enviable one. He seems to have made one or two attempts to be accepted again by the other Jews, who did not actually banish him and treat him as an outlaw as they had been exhorted to do. But he was accepted by modest Christian groups who had themselves thrown off harsh and oppressive ecclesiasticism. I do not mean that he formally adhered to these groups; he never became a Christian. I mean only that these clusters of pious, serious-minded folk, including a good many of superior learning and intelligence, welcomed him into their neighborhoods and homes, and gave him employment. They had suffered from the same excesses of priestly coercion that he had found in his own people.

He made his living grinding lenses. As his fame as a

scholar grew, he became intimate with some of the most
powerful men in the Dutch government, and two of them,
against his wishes, left legacies ample to his needs. His entire
life was passed in the parts of Holland lying roughly between
Amsterdam and Rotterdam; he refused an invitation to become a professor at Heidelberg, fearing that his liberty of
thought would be interfered with; but he maintained his
contact with the intellectual world through visitors (including the young philosopher Leibniz) and through his cor-
respondence with learned men throughout Europe. He died
of tuberculosis at the age of forty-four, in 1677.

I have made special mention of the cordial relations between the Jews and the Christians in Amsterdam. Still, we
must not think that there was much religious liberty. The
influence of the Calvinist clergy on the government was
strong and baneful; heresy and free thought were spied out
and denounced. Spinoza does not seem to have suffered any
special disabilities or dangers because he was a Jew; he had
enough to suffer because he thought his own thoughts and
spoke them out. His most important writing on religion had
to be published anonymously; but when its authorship became known, one theologian said "it was forged in hell by a
renegade Jew and the devil"—thereby illustrating the bigotry
the book was directed against. Spinoza then saw that his
chief philosophical work, the *Ethics*, could not receive a fair
hearing and might bring serious reprisals upon him. He
therefore kept it, with secret instructions for its publication
after his death.

In order to understand Spinoza's views on religion, we
must understand the relations between his *Theological-Political Tractate* and his *Ethics*. They were written on related
but different problems, for different audiences, and with different aims. The first book is on religion, where religion
means practices and institutions, and its purpose is to eradi-
cate abuses in religion and to bring it into what Spinoza

believed would be a sound system of political and social forces. The second is not a book on religion in this sense, but a metaphysical treatise on God and man in their relationships to each other; it presents Spinoza's philosophy as a substitute for religion based on revelation, tradition, and institutional forms.

The first of these books, the *Theological-Political Tractate*, is a polemical work, not a philosophical treatise serene above conflicting factions. The clergy had begun to make its will felt in various repressive measures; it had brought about the fall of Jan de Witt, a leader in the moderate government and Spinoza's friend; it had begun the banishment of Quakers and Mennonites and the removal of its own moderate members. The *Tractate*, published in 1670, was Spinoza's answer to their bigotry. The book was not, however, openly inflammatory; it was written in Latin, and addressed not to the general public, but to those among the learned to whom reason, or philosophy, had remained the handmaiden to theology and to whom, therefore, there was a theological warrant for interfering with the *libertas philosophandi*. The whole purpose of the work, he said, was to separate faith from philosophy so that each might go its own way, undisturbed by the other.

The book begins with a lengthy and detailed examination of the text of the Bible, an examination so influential as a model that Spinoza is now considered the father of Higher Criticism. It was nothing new, of course, to find inconsistencies in Scripture. Before Spinoza's time, two ways of resolving them had been practiced. One was to interpret some of the passages metaphorically, others literally. This method made reason, or philosophy, the rule in biblical criticism. The other was to accept the inconsistencies and to reject reason's competence to criticize them. The first way was based on the assumption that the Bible contains nothing that is philosophically false; the second was based on the assumption that it does, but says: so much the worse for human logic and philosophy.

Spinoza introduced a new way of dealing with this ancient problem. It is an extension of the first of the methods. He accepts the inconsistencies as real and asks two questions: (1) How did they arise? (2) What is their significance? To the first he answers that they arose because of the various circumstances in which the books were written, by very different men in different centuries, each faced with a specific moral or political situation, and each reflecting the culture of his time. Spinoza thus applied to Scripture the same techniques of interpretation that we would use in coming to an understanding of any other document written by many men under different conditions.

To the question "What is their significance?" Spinoza drew a very careful distinction between what the writers of the books meant and what they are taken to mean by bibliolaters of later times. It was here that he parted ways with the metaphor-hunters. He did not believe there was any reason to argue that they were always saying the same thing, sometimes clearly and directly, sometimes obscurely —often so obscurely that the untutored reader thinks that they were contradicting themselves. He said, rather, that the authors of the books had not been primarily concerned with teaching science or history or philosophy; in these fields they accepted the ideas current at their time. They were not devoted to teaching or increasing knowledge at all, but to teaching obedience. This they did in the only way they could and in the only way that could have had any hope of success, namely, by making use of the ideas accepted by their listeners and readers and, so far as we know, by themselves too. All the inconsistencies, Spinoza argued, arise from natural differences between the ideas of different ages and from differences in the authors' circumstances.

What most exercised the writers and prophets was persuading men to love their neighbors, to do justice, and to walk humbly with God. It was law and morals, not philosophy and science, that they were teaching. And in what they were teaching in this paramount sense, Spinoza found no inconsistencies at all. The meaning of this part of their message is clear, and it has come down to us uncorrupted by generations of scribes and commentators; it is as valid now as it was when it was first taught two or more thousand years ago. The teachings make a perfectly consistent body of what Spinoza called Divine Law, most of which could have been discovered by reason without the aid of prophecy. But since the majority of men do not reason philosophically, the way of learning by prophecy, miracle, and exhortation was vouchsafed to them.

The Divine Law is believed to be the ordinance of God revealed to the prophets and contained in Scripture. But since it is in substance the same as the law (the law of nature) which could be discovered by unaided reason, true religion requires nothing of man, either in belief or deed, which is different from that which a completely rational enlightened man would see to be right. These incorruptible truths of religion, which are embodied in, but must be distinguished from, the dogmatic formulae of specific religions, are consistently expounded in the Bible. They are: the existence, unity, omnipresence, and supremacy of God, together with three propositions bearing directly on the moral life:

That the worship of God consists only in justice and charity, or love toward one's neighbor.
That all those, and those only, who obey God by their manner of life are saved; the rest of mankind, who live under the sway of their pleasures, are lost. . . .
That God forgives the sins of those who repent.[2]

Theologians and ecclesiastics, however, have not put the emphasis in the right place in their teachings. There are

schisms and persecutions resulting from disagreements on
the interpretation of peripheral points of history, science, and
philosophy which have no divine sanction and no importance to upright living. In the excessive zeal they display in
stamping out interpretations with which they disagree, they
themselves sin most grievously against the basic religious and
moral doctrines, about which there is not any doubt or dispute at all.

This unseemly and unchristian disputation and persecution, Spinoza continued, disturbs the public peace and welfare. Such open warfare among the sects does not manifest
freedom of religion; on the contrary, it is a great threat to
such freedom, since one group of men harasses another, not
for their way of living (which is as blameless as their own),
but for their very thoughts.

To end it, Spinoza proposed a solution that may sound
like a paradox: it is to secure freedom within a state church.
First, he said, since it is the responsibility of the state to
preserve domestic quiet, and since peace is threatened or
destroyed by warring ecclesiastical bands, the authority of
the state in matters of public religion should be sovereign.
The aim of religion is to secure obedience to Divine Law; the
aim of the state is to secure obedience to the law of nature,
which is perfectly consistent with Divine Law. Hence the
state should have authority to establish churches and to
regulate their discipline so as to prevent them from disturb-
ing the body politic.

But second, the state should at the same time guarantee
to the citizenry something impossible under ecclesiastical
usurpation of political power: the freedom to think what
they will and to say what they think.

The ultimate aim of government is not to rule, or restrain,
by fear, nor to exact obedience, but contrariwise, to free every
man from fear, that he may live in all possible security; in other
words, to strengthen his natural right to exist and work without

injury to himself or others. No, the object of government is not to change men from rational beings into beasts and puppets, but to enable them to develop their minds and bodies in security, and to employ their reason unshackled. . . . In fact, the true aim of government is liberty.[3]

Such liberty is not just a concession to the citizenry; Spinoza argued that it is essential to the welfare of the government and society itself. Laws which restrict freedom of thought and speech cannot, in fact, be enforced, and the attempt to enforce them creates a rebellious state of mind in which the fruits of thought are denied to the state itself:

Men, as generally constituted, are most prone to resent the branding as criminal of opinions which they believe to be true, and the proscription as wicked of that which inspires them with piety towards God and man; hence they are ready to forswear the laws and conspire against the authorities, thinking it not shameful but honorable to stir up seditions and perpetrate any sort of crime with this end in view. Such being the constitution of human nature, we see that laws directed against opinions affect the generous-minded instead of the wicked, and are adapted less for coercing criminals than for irritating the up-right; so that they cannot be maintained without grave peril to the state.[4]

And he concluded with a historical proof of what he had said by citing the prosperity and culture of Amsterdam and the happiness and virtue of its citizens before the outbreak of the religious quarrels.

To the *Apology* of Plato, Locke's *Letters concerning Toleration*, Milton's *Areopagitica*, Kant's *What is Enlightenment?*, and Mill's *On Liberty*, we must add Spinoza's *Tractate* as one of the most powerful and eloquent arguments for freedom of thought and speech.

I come now to Spinoza's *magnum opus*, one of the greatest philosophical works of all time, the full title of which is *Ethics, Demonstrated in a Geometrical Manner*. Spinoza took mathematics as the model for the style of this work, believing that mathematical clarity and mathematical certainty were possible in philosophy. Accordingly, we find in the *Ethics* axioms, definitions, postulates, propositions with their proofs, and corollaries, just as in a geometrical treatise. Spinoza believed that he could deduce necessary truths about God, the world, human nature, vice and virtue from self-evident rational principles.

Two fundamental traits of Spinoza's philosophy—either one of which seems hopelessly at variance with a religious outlook—are his mechanism and his monism. Mechanism is the doctrine that whatever occurs in the universe takes place by causal necessity under the laws of nature. Things happen as they do because other things have already happened in the manner and at the place and time they did happen, and science is the body of knowledge of these necessary connections between them. In a mechanistic world-view, there is no place for explanations of things in terms of their purposes or value; there is no chance, and no capricious freedom of the will. Men believe they are free only because they are ignorant of the causes that determine their actions. When they ascribe some fortunate event to chance or to the will of God, they are confessing merely that they do not understand it; the will of God, said Spinoza, is "the sanctuary of ignorance."[5] Men do not act for the purpose of realizing some objective good; good and evil are mere ideas in the mind, and we call things good only because we desire them, and do not desire them because we find that they are good. All nature, including human nature and its aspirations, is thus laid open by the philosophy of mechanism to scientific dissection and mathematical computation. There is no mystery, but only ignorance; there are no miracles, but only events the ignorant do not understand under the laws of nature; there is no purpose and no providential hand of God anywhere in the universe, but all events occur and all things exist under the laws of mechanical and logical necessity.

Monism is the name of the philosophy which says that reality is one and that the variety of things apparent to us is not basic but is only an appearance of some underlying unity. Spinoza's philosophy is monistic. The underlying reality is called substance. Substance, however, is not a kind of matter or matter itself; rather it has some of the attributes normally ascribed to God: it is infinite, eternal, omnipresent, and self-sufficient. It is the explanation and cause of all other things, which are only manifestations of its nature. It is not personal, though Spinoza called it God. We do not see it as it is in itself, but only as it must appear to a being like ourselves.

It appears to us under two aspects, or attributes, though it actually has an infinite number of different attributes we cannot conceive. The attributes we know are space and thought. Under the attribute of space, substance is understood as the physical world, infinite in extension, in which all motions occur under the laws of physics. Under the aspect of thought, substance appears as mind, in which thoughts and feelings occur under the laws of psychology and logic. The physical and the mental are two perspectives under which we contemplate the one ultimate substance, God, which is neither intrinsically physical nor intrinsically mental; body and mind are appearances of one reality. They do not influence each other, but whatever happens in one is reflected in what happens in the other.

If there is anything miraculous in such a world, it is the near-miracle that a religious and moral philosophy could be built upon this conception of it. Yet this is what Spinoza performed. Montague writes:

Who, moreover, can remain unmoved at the spectacle of its author, the outcast Jew of quiet courage, the lonely man without a country, who wrought the vision [of such a world] and then with all the ardor of a Christian saint took the bleak thing to his own bleak heart, called it God, and in its cold embrace found peace?[6]

I shall now try to show briefly, and with an admitted oversimplification, how Spinoza did find peace in this bleak conception, how it satisfied the quest which he set out upon in the opening sentences of *On the Improvement of the Understanding.*

We have already seen how, in his *Tractate,* Spinoza identified the content of Divine Law with that of the moral law, or the law of nature established by reason. While religion emphasizes the divine origin of our knowledge of what ought to be, and regards God as a moral lawgiver, philosophy does not depend for its knowledge of moral or natural law upon revelation, nor does it regard the law as being dependent upon the will of God. Indeed, in Spinoza's philosophy, there is no "will of God" except in a metaphorical sense, for God is not a personal being. Philosophy bases its conception of the law upon knowledge of nature and human nature, which, when fully elaborated, leads to the conception of God as substance and not as personality. The philosophical conception of God is thus wholly free from the anthropomorphic elements so important in popular religion; and the emotional, personal relation the religious person feels toward God and expresses in such acts as prayer and praise must be, for the philosopher, replaced by a more intellectual, objective conception of the relation of man to an impersonal but all-embracing reality.

The truths of religion and their ethical consequences, therefore, correspond to, but are not identical with, the metaphysical truths and their consequences. For example, Spinoza spoke in the *Tractate* of "forgiveness of sin," which men gain by the grace of God secured through repentance. But the God of Spinoza's philosophy is not a person and cannot forgive, and it is hard to justify repentance for acts which a person could not have failed to commit. Still, the religious truth of salvation through repentance has a philosophical counterpart, and may be regarded as a popular metaphor for it. The philosophical truth is that men, by widening their vision and seeing themselves in relation to substance *sub specie aeternitatis*, are no longer attracted by those things that assail their true nature, detract from their essential being and destiny, and seduce them from the path of wisdom. The turn from human vanity to wisdom, celebrated in the *Improvement*, is a secularized version of the sense of sin and rebirth through a larger vision promising a freer and more contented life. Hence even in his philosophical ethics, Spinoza is not contradicting the popular version of religious morals he had given in the *Tractate*.

Another illustration. Salvation does not mean the same thing philosophically as religiously. Philosophically it does not mean getting to heaven or enjoying the personal presence of a loving God; it means seeing ourselves as we really are, which means seeing ourselves in relation to the world-whole, and not distorting our picture of the cosmos as though it turned about ourselves or had been created by God for our benefit and edification. The path to salvation, which in religion is the love of God, has also a philosophical complement in our satisfied conception of our status in the world-whole. This is what Spinoza called the *amor intellectualis dei*, the intellectual love of God.

To trace out this path to "salvation" is the subject matter of the last two books of the *Ethics*, which are entitled "Of Human Bondage" and "Of Human Freedom." Pleasure, he says, is the feeling we have when we pass from a lower to a higher degree of perfection. We have this feeling whenever the natural functioning of the mind or body is enhanced. Thus, improvement in health, which is a natural adjustment of the body to the world, is accompanied by pleasure, and in advancing in knowledge and insight we improve the power

of the mind and find a delight in it. Love he defines as the
feeling of pleasure accompanied by our knowledge of its
cause. The increase in our understanding is always accompanied with the feeling of pleasure and, therefore, with love
for that which brings us this pleasure.

We do not know anything fully until we see it in relation
to ultimate reality, the reason and cause of all things, which
is substance, or God. Therefore, the person who sees things
under the aspect of eternity necessarily feels love for the
cause of this joy, which can come only with our knowing
God. This is the intellectual love of God. Such love of the
eternal and necessary frees us from our ordinary subjection
to the changeable things, in the temporary possession of
which there is no lasting satisfaction. Through our love of
God, we are rescued from human bondage, which is the
love of things of the flesh and of things temporal and uncertain. Guided by our knowledge of God, we gladly do
actions required by the laws of morals and of nature, which
are now, in a sense deeper than that of the popular religion,
laws of God. These actions constitute virtue. Virtue does
not lead to happiness as something different from itself, to
be enjoyed later, perhaps in heaven. The actions of a virtuous
man are themselves done with joy. "Blessedness is not the
reward of virtue, but virtue itself."

Here, then, is the philosophical religion of Spinoza, the
kind of religion to be practiced not by the masses in churches
established by the state, but the kind to be practiced by the
philosopher who thinks his own thought in freedom. It is the
religion of the wise man. Spinoza concluded his great work
with the words:

The wise man . . . is scarcely at all disturbed in spirit; but,
being conscious of himself, and of God, and of things, by a certain eternal necessity . . . always possesses true acquiescence of
his spirit. If the way which I have pointed out as leading to this
result seems exceeding hard, it may nevertheless be discovered.

Needs must it be hard, since it is so seldom found. How would it be possible, if salvation were ready to our hand, and could without great labor be found, that it should be by almost all men neglected? But all things excellent are as difficult as they are rare.[7]

Suggested Readings

The *Ethics* exists in many editions; there is a paperback edition edited by James H. Gutmann in the Hafner Library of Classics. The *Theological-Political Tractate* has been published less widely, but it is now available in *The Political Works of Spinoza*, translated by A. G. Wernam (Oxford: Clarendon Press, 1958).

The most exhaustive and penetrating study of Spinoza is H. A. Wolfson's *The Philosophy of Spinoza* (Cambridge: Harvard University Press, 1934; one-volume paperback edition by Meridian Books, New York). The fullest study of Spinoza's relation to religion is perhaps E. E. Powell's *Spinoza and Religion* (Boston: Chapman and Grimes, 1941). The chapters on Spinoza in Montague, *op. cit.*, and in Burtt's *Types of Religious Philosophy*, are recommended.

Lewis Browne's *Blessed Spinoza* (New York: Macmillan and Co., 1932) gives a popular, somewhat romanticized account of Spinoza's life. E. G. Kolbenheyer's *God-Intoxicated Man* (London: Ivor Nicholson and Watson, 1933) is a novel based on Spinoza's life.

IV

Hume

David Hume, the greatest of all the British philosophers, was born in Edinburgh in 1711 and died there in 1776. His position in the intellectual life of his time was important. Next to Gibbon he was the greatest historian of his century, and next to Dr. Johnson he was the most notable literary figure of the latter part of the century. The clergy of Scotland hated what he stood for, yet some of his best friends were clergymen. His opponents said that his philosophy could best be summarized in an epigram of Lady Mary Wortley Montagu's—"Take the 'not' out of the Decalogue and put it in the Creed"—yet his character was so good and his person so amiable that he was honored and loved. Boswell was incredulously shocked that so godless a man could live so well and die so fearlessly; but Adam Smith, who also knew him well, wrote:

> I have always considered him, both in his lifetime and since his death, as approaching as nearly to the idea of a perfectly wise and virtuous man as perhaps the nature of human frailty will permit.[1]

The word "agnosticism" was coined in the nineteenth century by Thomas Henry Huxley to name his own view of religion. It means the position that holds both the assertion and the denial of religious doctrines to be unfounded on sufficient evidence. It is not the same as atheism, for that is the positive assertion that God does not exist, and the

42

agnostic says simply we do not know whether He exists or not. Agnosticism is skepticism in religious matters. Hume did often say that God exists; but his statements are so hedged in with qualifications and reservations, and in the light of the rest of his philosophy he had so little reason for making them, that most students of Hume have not hesitated to call him a religious skeptic and, in spite of the anachronism, an agnostic.

The best word to describe Hume's philosophy as a whole, however, is "empiricism." An empiricist believes that our knowledge arises from sense experience and can be known to be correct only when it can be checked against future experience. Pure reason, which the rationalists like Spinoza trusted, is valid in logic and mathematics, Hume says, because we are there concerned only with the relations of our ideas to each other. We can know by reason that if a certain figure is a triangle, its angles necessarily equal two right angles; but reason is incapable of deciding questions of fact, such as: Is this a triangle? To answer questions about what is really existent in the world, the empiricist teaches that reason must start with the data of the senses, work with them to derive conclusions, and check the conclusions by further observation.

Even this, however, will not give us certain knowledge. All our knowledge of matters of fact except memories and reports on our immediate experience (e.g., "I am now in pain") depend upon inferences from our immediate experience to something else. All these inferences depend upon the principle of causation. But what does one mean when he says, for instance, "Fire causes the pot to boil"? If he says that all his knowledge comes from experience, he must mean only that in all the cases he has observed, putting the pot on the fire has been followed by the water's boiling, and that he expects it to happen again and again. This expectation is not based upon a knowledge merely of the relations among our ideas, and it is not an expectation that can be justified by past experience because it refers to *future* experience. It can be justified only by waiting for the experience it foretells, and it may in some or all future cases be disappointed. But suppose our prediction is confirmed the next time we see a pot on the stove; still, the next time we make a prediction we shall be in the same situation all over again. Hence all our knowledge of the course of nature is at best only probable.

The alleged truths of metaphysical and theological speculation are neither logically necessary, nor derived from experience, nor testable in experience. If Hume is correct, therefore, they are not knowledge at all; they lie wholly beyond the sphere of the competence of the human mind.

Hume was perfectly aware of the revolutionary consequences of his theory of knowledge, and he concludes his *Enquiry Concerning Human Understanding* with these uncompromising words:

When we run over libraries, persuaded of these principles, what havoc must we make? If we take in our hand any volume, —of divinity or school metaphysics, for instance—let us ask, *does it contain any abstract reasoning concerning quantity and number* [relations of ideas]? No. *Does it contain any experimental* [i.e., empirical] *reasoning concerning matter of fact and existence?* No. Commit it then to the flames: for it can contain nothing but sophistry and illusion.[2]

This is a direct challenge to all those who believed either in the pure reasonableness of religion or in the validity of reasoning from our knowledge of nature to God.

The second of these challenges is the more important. The eighteenth century is sometimes called the Age of Reason, but it was not an Age of Pure Reason. The typical eighteenth-century thinker in England had given up most of the claims of platonism and rationalism and was insistent upon the necessity of observing and collecting empirical facts as an essential part of the life of reason. Hume was in agreement with this view that the only way to real knowledge was through reasoning on given facts, and not through pure reason and least of all through inspiration, revelation, or blind acts of faith. Theologians before Hume had themselves made a continuous effort to cut down the mysterious element in Christianity and to deny the necessity of accepting scriptural or ecclesiastical authority; they had done so in favor of emphasizing the essential reasonableness of Christianity, somewhat in the manner of Spinoza. Followers of Spinoza's rationalism, and empiricists prior to Hume, such as Locke, had argued that religion, and especially English Protestant religion, was founded on facts that anyone could see and on inferences that every reasonable man must make.

This doctrine of the reasonableness of Christianity is what Hume most insistently denied. Those who had undertaken to defend Christianity by the principles of reason, he said, are its "dangerous friends or disguised enemies," for "our most holy religion is founded on faith, not on reason; and it is a sure method of exposing it to put it to such a trial [of reason] as it is by no means fitted to endure.[3] To say that it is founded on faith and not on reason was, in the climate of opinion at that time, almost the same as to say that it was founded on nothing at all. But by saying this, the canny Scot exculpated himself from the charge of irreligion while he girded himself to deliver one of the most stunning attacks on religion that has ever been made.

What, then, are the evidences cited by those who believe theology to be a reasonable system of ideas or a reasonable interpretation of observed facts? Hume considered three in detail: the occurrence of miracles, the order and harmony of nature, and the common consent of mankind.

The great majority believe that the best evidence for religion is extraordinary events which are supposed by them to show the direct intervention of God in the course of history and nature. Such interventions are miracles. Hume's problem was to find out whether a reasonable man should believe that they actually occur. He regarded this as an empirical question. Being a historian, he saw it as a problem of weighing historical evidence. This was an entirely different approach from that of Spinoza, who disbelieved in miracles because he accepted the theory of the mechanistic order of nature. A metaphysical answer would not satisfy Hume; he wanted an empirical answer, for he saw that the mechanistic theory is itself false if miracles do in fact occur.

 But when he examined the empirical origin of our conception of the uniformity of nature, he saw that this was evidence against the occurrence of miracles. We discover laws of nature by repeated observation of the same kinds of events happening over and over again under like conditions. This does not logically prove that nature is uniform in all her parts; but the accumulation of such generalizations strengthens our conviction that she is uniform. A law of nature is an expression merely of the most probable order of events, but this probability is practically as good as a certainty.

A miracle is, by definition, a violation of a law of nature. It is not an event which is unexplained merely by the laws we have already discovered; the world is full of such events, and they show only the magnitude of our ignorance, not the hand of God. No, a miracle is an event inexplicable by any law of nature, discovered or yet to be discovered. It is, therefore, an event which would have to be judged to be improbable no matter how much we knew. A man who believes in miracles, therefore, not only believes in the power of God, but also disbelieves in the power of human reason to explain much of what is as yet unexplained.

The probabilities are always against the occurrence of a miracle; this follows simply from the definition, since a law of nature, of which a miracle is a violation, is a statement of the highest probability we have been able to ascertain. This does not show that miracles are impossible; it merely shows that the evidence for them must be overwhelmingly strong if it is to count against the great antecedent improbability of the event.

Since the laws of nature are highly probable and the occurrence of a miracle is highly improbable, and since anything that increases the probability of the one lowers the probability of the other, Hume set up a rule for the weighing of evidence of miracles. It was: "No testimony is sufficient to establish a miracle unless the testimony be of such a kind that its falsehood would be more miraculous than the fact which it endeavors to establish."[4]

This is the rule the historian uses in weighing evidence. Two contemporary documents conflict with each other: one document says Napoleon died in 1821, another says he was seen in Louisiana in 1826. Which is the more probable: that both are true or that at least one of the documents is mistaken? The answer is obvious. Now which is the more miraculous: that the sun should have stood still while Joshua's men finished slaughtering their foe or that the narrator has made a mistake? Hume thought the answer to this question was equally obvious.

We know enough about astronomy to infer that the stopping of the sun is exceedingly improbable; we know enough about human nature to infer that a false report of what happened during a great battle is not at all improbable. We know how even honest folk will occasionally embellish a tale to make a better story, for love of wonder and a delight in astonishing others are natural to man:

But if the spirit of religion join itself to the love of wonder, there is an end of common sense; and human testimony, in these circumstances, loses all pretensions to authority. A religionist may be an enthusiast, and imagine he sees what has no reality;

he may know his narrative to be false, and yet persevere in it
with the best intentions in the world for the sake of promoting
so holy a cause. Or even where this delusion has not place, vanity,
excited by so strong a temptation, operates on him more power-
fully than on the rest of mankind in other circumstances; and
self-interest with equal force. His auditors may not have, and
commonly have not, sufficient judgment to canvass his evidence;
what judgment they have, they renounce by principle in these
sublime and mysterious subjects. Of if they were ever willing
to employ it, passion and a heated imagination disturb the regularity of its operations. Their credulity increases his impudence;
and his impudence overpowers their credulity.[5]

Applying, then, the ordinary canons of historical method
and this realistic estimate of human frailty, Hume concluded
that

there is not to be found, in all history, any miracle attested by
a sufficient number of men of such unquestioned good sense,
education, and learning, as to secure us against all delusion in
themselves; of such undoubted integrity as to place them beyond
all suspicion of any design to deceive others; of such credit and
reputation in the eyes of mankind as to have a great deal to lose
in case of their being detected in any falsehood, and at the same
time attesting facts performed in such a public manner and in
so celebrated a part of the world as to render detection unavoid-
able.[6]

Hume believed that the acceptance of miracles is a poor
foundation for religion, also, because the belief in them pre-
vents us from making use of better evidence for the existence
of God. This evidence is the presence of design and order
in the majestic machine of nature. One cannot honestly
appeal to this as the handiwork of a perfect Author of
Nature endowed with omniscience and omnipotence and at
the same time believe that the unusual, the inexplicable, the
miraculous, show that there is a god intervening in the
course of the nature He has established. If miracles occur

and have any religious significance, they must indicate that
there is a Particular Providence intervening to rectify nature
for man's benefit or edification; if the order of nature exists
and has any religious significance, it must indicate that there
is a General Providence which established and now sustains
nature in her awesome magnitude without the necessity of
divine afterthoughts of particular miraculous intervention in
the orderly course of nature. You cannot have it both ways,
says Hume: order or intervention, but not both. And Hume
thought that the argument from order was incomparably the
better.

His analysis of the better argument is found in his
posthumous work, *Dialogues Concerning Natural Religion*.
Natural religion means religious, or rather theological, beliefs
based on the facts of nature, especially as they are disclosed
in scientific discovery. The most important of the evidences
is the order and harmony of nature, which is taken to indicate
intelligent and beneficent design. Natural theology is con-
trasted to revealed theology, which is based on particular
revelations in the Bible or in miracles or in the private revelations claimed by individuals, all of which speak to our faith
instead of our reason. Natural theology, therefore, had a
pre-eminent place in the cool Age of Reason, which was re-
acting against the obscurantism of an Age of Faith.

It is not possible, in a paraphrase or brief summary, to
do justice to the *Dialogues*. One can summarize the arguments and conclusions of most of Hume's philosophical
works, and regret only that in the summary the sharpness
and wit of the style are lost; but one can hardly give even a
résumé of the arguments and conclusions of the *Dialogues*,
for there is not one straight line of argument leading to an
inevitable conclusion. That such discourse is especially appropriate in a matter like religion, where Hume thought no
certainty is possible, is acknowledged in the fact that this
work was not composed as a treatise; it is a dialogue in which

the various pieces are not spoken by mere abstract represent-
atives of well-established and sharply defined views, nor are
all the victories won by the spokesman for the author. The
three speakers—Demea, Cleanthes, and Philo—are lifelike,
and as their discussion develops, the lines of demarkation
between their developing views often become somewhat obscure, as in a real conversation in which each man learns
from the others, modifies his own views to take account of
theirs, and joins and unjoins temporary alliances with one
or more of his fellow speakers. Nevertheless, each of the men
does have an ax to grind: Demea is an orthodox rationalist,
using arguments for the existence and nature of God not
unlike those of Spinoza, and holding to the rational certainty of his religious dogmas. Cleanthes is a natural theologian who infers the high probability of the existence of
God from the evidences of design in nature. Philo is a skeptic
who criticizes both, but often sides with Cleanthes, against
Demea, as being the less dogmatic.

One would normally assume that Philo is Hume's spokesman in these *Dialogues,* and certainly there is more of the
Hume we know from his other works in the speeches of
Philo than in those of the others. Yet the narrator of the
Dialogues, Pamphilus, surprisingly treats Cleanthes as the
hero, and statements we hardly expect to hear from Hume
are put into Philo's mouth. Hume was too good a literary
craftsman for us to assume that these puzzles for the inter-
preter are due to any carelessness on his part, so we have
to assume that these puzzles have a purpose. I do not believe
that one can seriously maintain that when these *Dialogues*
were written, Hume was himself wavering in his skeptical
attitude towards religion, or that he wished to hide his
views from the reader—after all, he had already exacerbated
his orthodox readers again and again; and although he found
polemics distasteful, he did not plan to publish this work in
his lifetime.

The explanation for the puzzle is perhaps this. It is unseemly for a skeptic to take the role of a dogmatist, even of a dogmatic skeptic, who should preserve an open mind. And there is a dramatic and polemical purpose in presenting his views as if they were a joint product of at least two of his speakers, Philo and Cleanthes, and agreeable to both. Even so, the fact that the existence of God is said not to be the question, but only His nature, and the fact that Philo concedes at the end that there probably is a Designer of the world having some resemblance to the human mind— a point he has attacked repeatedly—make these *Dialogues* a puzzling document for the understanding of Hume himself.

The classical argument from design, which we find at least as far back as the Psalms and Plato, is stated by Cleanthes at the beginning of the second *Dialogue*:

Look round the world: contemplate the whole and every part of it: You will find it to be nothing but one great machine, subdivided into an infinite number of lesser machines, which again admit of subdivisions, to a degree beyond what human senses and faculties can trace and explain. All these various machines, and even their most minute parts, are adjusted to each other with an accuracy which ravishes into admiration all men, who have ever contemplated them. The curious adapting of means to end, throughout all nature, resembles exactly, though it much exceeds, the productions of human contrivance; of human design, thought, wisdom, and intelligence. Since therefore the effects resemble each other, we are led to infer, by all the rules of analogy, that the causes also resemble; and that the Author of Nature is somewhat similar to the mind of man; though possessed of much larger faculties, proportioned to the grandeur of the work which he has executed.[7]

However convincing the argument is at first glance, and however much conviction it carries even after it has been criticized—and both Hume and Kant, its chief critics, acknowledged that it is effective and worthy of respect even when its faults are exposed—Hume found much in it to arouse his suspicion and irony. The analogy it draws between the world and God, on the one hand, and a machine and its builder, on the other, is no better than analogies between the world and a work of art or a ship or a house or a biological offspring; and from these analogies we get, by the same argument, the concept of God as an artist, an architect, a parent, and the like. Unless we have some prior conception of God which does not come from the observation of nature, we do not know which of the possible analogies to prefer. We simply do not know what is most typical in the structure of the world.

We know far too little of nature as a whole to reason, with any assurance, from the part of it we do know to the whole. We know that "stone, wood, brick, iron, brass, have not, at this time, in this minute globe of earth, an order or arrangement without human art and contrivance: . . ."[8] but from that, Philo says, we cannot infer that all arrangement is due to anything like the human mind. In the vast spaces and times of the universe, may not matter organize itself? This question was asked by Hume, who was ignorant of Kant's attempt, made just a few years earlier, to explain the order of the solar system by reference to Newton's laws of motion and without the hypothesis of design; the Kant-Laplace hypothesis is a hypothesis as to how indeed the matter of the nebula could have organized itself into the solar system, which has always been one of the exhibits for the argument from design. Because we technologically organize matter by the use of our intelligence and skill is no reason to suppose that all organization has mind as its cause; to suppose that it does is as sophistical as "the narrow views of a peasant, who makes his domestic economy the rule for the government of kingdoms. . . ."[9]

All such arguments, which begin with the grand sublimity

of the astronomical universe, end in a mean and paltry conception of the deity, an anthropomorphism* which is no more intelligible and plausible and far less expressive of religious humility than the conception (like Spinoza's) that organization is native to the universe itself. But if we are honest in our analogizing, the anthropomorphic conception of deity does not explain anything finally; it rather leads us into an infinite regress, in which the conception of a designer is no closer to the final answer than the conception of a universe that designs itself. For consider: we find in ourselves that our minds—the only ones we know—are affected by all sorts of conditions lying outside our power, in things before us and outside us; and hence we have no right, under the analogy, to assume as a cause of the world order a mind which in this respect is wholly unlike the only minds we know. Of this divine mind, just as of our own, we would have to be able to ask, "What caused *it?*" This is not a question which the believer in God as a first cause can ask; but if he reaches this conception by an analogical argument from what does have a cause, it is a question he ought to ask.

We have spoken of the so-called natural attributes of God, those by which He is supposed to be the author of the physical order. But what about the moral order, or the order of values? Those who argue by analogy in favor of a beneficent God, as the Christian natural theologians do, proceed only by dishonestly stacking the cards in His favor. They choose only those parts of nature which do suggest wise and merciful Providence, and neglect those other parts which, to the impartial eye, suggest that the world was not designed

* Philo asks: "And why not become a perfect Anthropomorphite? Why not assert the deity or deities to be corporeal, and to have eyes, a nose, mouth, ears, etc.? EPICURUS maintained, that no man had ever seen reason but in a human figure; therefore the gods must have a human figure. And this argument, which is deservedly so much ridiculed by Cicero, becomes, according to you [Cleanthes], solid and philosophical."[10]

for human benefit. There is pestilence and evil and agony
in the world, as well as beauty and harmony and happiness.
If we are to ascribe it all to the work of one omnipotent God,
the evil in the world will be incompatible with our conception of His goodness; if we attribute perfect goodness to
God, the evil will cause us to question His power. If we
argue from the order and harmony of nature to a wise and
beneficent Creator, ought we not, in honesty, to argue by a
like analogy from apparent disorder and evil to an evil
creator or to a powerful opponent of God?

Believing, on some other grounds, that there is an omnipotent and perfect Creator, theologians in dealing with the
problem of Job can give us many ingenious explanations of
the evil in the world that are consistent with this theological
hypothesis. For example, there is the doctrine that by the
grace of God the evil will be made good in some mysterious
way that is beyond human comprehension. Hume grants
this possibility. But until the existence of such a God has
been established, we have to accept the evil along with the
good and give equal weight to whatever we find in the
world, be it good or evil.

We ought to argue only for those attributes of God which
are necessary and sufficient to explain the facts as we find
them, let the facts be what they may. If we do so, the immense variety of analogies possible from the infinite variety
of things in the world contributes nothing to the conception
of one God; the argument from the designs in the world,
which are not all alike, is more favorable to polytheism than
to monotheism. Moreover, we cannot argue in this way to
the conception of a perfect God; the deity whose existence
is proved by analogy must be just sufficient to explain the
facts, not a bit more. But apart from the prior conception
of God as a perfect being, which has not been proved, we
have no reason to think that this world could not have

been created except by a perfect being, because we do not know that this is the best of all possible worlds:

> This world, for aught [we know] is very faulty and imperfect, compared to a superior standard; and was only the first rude essay of some infant deity, who afterwards abandoned it, ashamed of his lame performance; it is the work only of some dependent, inferior deity; and is the object of derision to his superiors: it is the production of old age and dotage in some superannuated deity; and ever since his death, has run on at adventures, from the first impulse and active force, which it received from him.[11]

Hume's final verdict on the argument from design, however, was surprising in its mildness. He concludes—though it is hard to see why—that the world arose from something like design, that the designer may have some remote resemblance to the human mind, but that he resembles man intellectually more than morally. Nevertheless, such inferences are far too uncertain to carry any religious weight; they do not have the certitude that the religious person claims for his beliefs. The proper attitude for the thinker, therefore, is one of cool reserve, of cautiously fitting his beliefs to the narrow shape of the evidence, of not trying to squeeze more out of the evidence than can be honestly got. If there is to be comfort and certitude in religious sentiment, it cannot come from an impartial examination of the evidence. "To be a philosophical Skeptic is, in a man of letters, the first and essential step towards being a sound, believing Christian,"[12] he concluded, because if a man is not a skeptic, if he holds, on the contrary, that reason working on the data of experience can establish true answers to religious questions, these answers will *not* be the answers required by Christian theology. The only honest attitude for the Christian, therefore, is one of faith, not one of claiming to base orthodox belief upon reason.

This does not mean that Hume favors faith above reason; it means only that if you insist upon being religious, you cannot appeal to reason to back up your faith. So for the second time Hume ironically and in a somewhat backhanded way seems to recommend faith beyond the sphere of reason's competence.

The third kind of evidence for the theological beliefs was the appeal to the common consent of mankind. The Platonists and deists argued that in the consciousness of every man and in every people there is an innate religious sentiment focused upon universally valid truths of religion, but that these have become obscured and perverted by the machinations and enthusiasms of sectarian priests. They therefore believed that if one could get away from all the pious hocus-pocus of theology and ritual, one would discover within himself the lineaments of a pure and reasonable belief in God.

While Hume was not in the least convinced of the validity of the fanciful elaborations of belief by subtle theologians, he was even less inclined to settle for this primitivistic appeal to unenlightened and uncultivated mankind. So he published, in 1757, his *Natural History of Religion*. The questions in this book are partly anthropological, partly philosophical, partly ethical. They are: What, in fact, was the religion of primitive man? Why did primitive men have the beliefs they had, and what caused them to change their beliefs? How much of this primitive religion is left after the chicanery of theologians is exposed?

Hume answered, correctly, that the original religion of mankind was not the reasonable religion of the deists, but polytheism of the most gross anthropomorphic kind. Primitive men believed in many gods, each of whom was a personification or even a caricature of some human trait, more often vicious than virtuous. Primitive gods were mysterious beings who thwarted or aided some human passion, often in ways ingenious and tricky. Hume does not explicitly say, but he surely believed, that men created the gods in their own image, and the divine image held by primitive man is nothing admirable or praiseworthy. Their gods were not models for human conduct, but fell notably behind the moral progress of many of their devotees, who often behaved better than their gods were believed to behave. They were not thought of as creators of the world or sustainers of the world order, but as meddlesome demons who had to be propitiated by magic and sacrifice in order to limit their nefarious caprices. Hume called primitive men "superstitious atheists," not innocent deists. In a word, the beliefs of primitive men were as far removed from what the deists were teaching as was the revealed theology the deists were opposing.

Only after long ages, and then only very incompletely, did more spiritual conceptions of deity gradually replace savage superstitiousness and idolatry. Even so, this improvement did not result from rational argument or from moral enlightenment, but mostly from the actions of men who took sides in the putative battles among the gods themselves. Broader sovereignty was thereby won for the gods of the victorious tribes, and thus monotheism gradually replaced polytheism through the instrumentality of war. The transition from gross anthropomorphism to a spiritual and ethical conception of God is late and slow and even yet incomplete and precarious. We still easily fall back into primitive ways of thinking of how we should please our gods:

If we should suppose, what never happens, that a popular religion were found, in which it was expressly declared, that nothing but morality could gain the divine favour; if an order of priests were instituted to inculcate this opinion, in daily sermons, and with all the arts of persuasion; yet so inveterate are the people's prejudices, that, for want of some other superstition, they would make the very attendance on these sermons the essentials of religion, rather than place them in virtue and good morals.[13]

It is not likely that the irony of this was missed by the clergy.

May we pride ourselves on having outgrown the grosser forms of religious superstition? No doubt; but still, other-worldly religion does two evil things to human morals. For actions which grow out of human nature and are approved by man's social sympathies, it tries to substitute Carthusian virtues and does not give any sanction or help to those things which make ordinary human life decent:

> In restoring a loan, or paying a debt, [a man's conception of] divinity is nowise beholden to him; because these acts of justice are what he was bound to perform, and what many would have performed, were there no god in the universe. But if he fast a day, or give himself a sound whipping; this has a direct reference, in his opinion, to the service of God. No other motive could engage him to such austerities. By these distinguished marks of devotion, he has now acquired the divine favour; and may expect, in recompense, protection and safety in this world, and eternal happiness in the next.[14]

Religion not only leaves the ordinary conceptions of human decency unsupported; it subverts them, by directing men's devotion and their efforts and emulation towards a standard which falls below the best human standards, for the religious standard was canonized in scripture in earlier, less-enlightened ages. Men's "gloomy apprehensions" make them ascribe to God "measures of conduct, which, in human creatures, would be highly blamed," and they must "affect to praise and admire that conduct in the object of their devotional addresses" which they would condemn if they met with it in society.[15] This makes for bigotry in the true believers, since "steady attention alone to so important an interest as that of eternal salvation is apt to extinguish the benevolent affections, and beget a narrow, contracted selfishness."[16] In the more enlightened whose standards are not sanctioned or recognized by religion, it begets hypocrisy if they wish to stay out of trouble.

This is Hume's chief criticism of popular religion; it is a moral, not a theoretical rebuke. So far from being a harmless thing, or even a useful device for controlling the ignorant masses, popular religion instills the wrong standard of morals. It puts the emphasis upon slavish attention to ritual details and turns men's minds away from those things that their natural sympathies or fellow-feeling would incline them to do if left undistorted by fear-inspiring mysteries and threats. Like his contemporary, Gibbon, therefore, Hume concluded that religion has been a misfortune in the history of mankind and has delayed and now delays moral as well as intellectual progress.

Surrounded by such vicious foolishness, therefore, the wise man will not be concerned with the disputes of theologians provided only he can make himself immune to their rancor and persecution. The vacuum left when he gives up religious convictions will be replaced by a cool contemplation of the world and of human folly. Like the Epicurean gods, he will withdraw from the furious battle:

Doubt, uncertainty, suspense of judgment appear the only result of our most accurate scrutiny, concerning this subject [of religion]. But such is the frailty of human reason, and such the irresistible contagion of religion, that even this deliberate doubt could scarcely be upheld; did we not enlarge our view, and opposing one species of superstition to another, set them a-quarreling; while we ourselves, during their fury and contention, happily make our escape into the calm, though obscure regions of philosophy.[17]

Suggested Readings

Most of Hume's writings are available in inexpensive editions. The volume *Hume Selections*, edited by Hendel, contains most of the relevant ones, though it omits the essay on miracles. Hendel has edited both the *Inquiry Concerning Human Understanding* and the *Inquiry Concerning the Principles of Morals* (New York: Liberal Arts Press, 1955 and 1957.) Henry D. Aiken has edited the *Dialogues Concerning Natural Religion* and a volume of selections, *Hume's Moral and Political Philosophy* in the series "Hafner Library of Classics" (New York: Hafner Publishing Co., 1948). Hume's little autobiography, together with Adam Smith's letter to Strahan, which I quoted in the text, can be found in the Open Court editions of the *Inquiry Concerning Human Understanding;* the autobiography alone is in Hendel's edition of the same work.

The best study of Hume's views on religion as a whole is given in the preface to Norman Kemp Smith's edition of the *Dialogues* (Oxford: Clarendon, 1935). The most interesting books on Hume's life and personality are both by E. C. Mossner: *The Forgotten Hume* (New York: Columbia University Press, 1943) and *The Life of David Hume* (Austin: The University of Texas Press, 1954 [also London: Nelson, 1954]).

V

Kant

Immanuel Kant was born in Königsberg, East Prussia, in 1724 and died there in 1804. He was a younger contemporary of Hume, whose works influenced him deeply. The other chief influences on his life came from science, from religion, and from one other man—Rousseau. Kant was greatly impressed by the development of science and was himself a competent physicist, astronomer, geologist, and mathematician. His name is remembered in science for his authorship of the nebular hypothesis, which is still known as the Kant-Laplace hypothesis. As an astronomical theory, it has been replaced by others, but its importance as a step in the history of astronomy can hardly be over estimated. In it Kant attempted to explain the origin of the solar system out of a primordial nebula, making use only of physical laws and without calling upon the intervention of God in nature; in essence, he said all explanation in science must be physical explanation, and if we have the thought of design at all, we may properly use it only as a guiding hypothesis in the discovery of physical causes.

The religious influence in Kant's life came from the sect known as the Pietists. Pietism was a religious movement in Germany somewhat like Methodism, which appeared later in England. The Pietists, or at least those Pietists close to Kant's own humble family, placed great and indeed almost exclusive emphasis upon upright behavior and simple faith, and they had no truck with ritualism or theological dispute.

Later, when he attended school, he was exposed to a more excessive kind of Pietism with an overemphasis upon public worship 'and on the depravity of little boys who did not gladly take to it; and it so bored and offended him that from that time on he never voluntarily entered a church and never had much good to say for the organized forms of religion, though he remained abreast of theological literature.

Rousseau's influence is chiefly seen in Kant's respect for the dignity of the common man, and in his political theory, which is strongly republican. He was a partisan of both the French and American Revolutions, at a time when to favor either was to bring suspicion upon oneself in Germany.

The German writer Herder had been a pupil of Kant's; many years later, after their disagreement on philosophical matters had embittered their relationship, Herder still expressed his veneration for his teacher, and said:

I have had the good fortune to know a philosopher. He was my teacher. In his prime he had the sprightliness of a youth; he continued to have it, I believe, even as a very old man. His broad forehead, built for thinking, was the seat of an imperturbable cheerfulness and joy. Speech, the richest in thought, flowed from his lips. Playfulness, wit, and humor were at his command. . . . The history of men and peoples, natural history and science, mathematics and observation, were the sources from which he enlivened his lectures and conversation. He was indifferent to nothing worth knowing. No cabal, no sect, no prejudice, no desire for fame could ever tempt him in the slightest from broadening and illuminating the truth. He incited and gently forced others to think for themselves; despotism was foreign to his mind. This man, whom I name with the greatest respect and gratitude, was Immanuel Kant.[1]

That is high praise, and no doubt to be taken more seriously in coming from a great man who was opposed to the Kantian philosophy.

Kant's life was calm and uneventful. Everyone knows the

story that the housewives of Königsberg set their clocks by
his regular daily walk. Heine said that his life passed with the
regularity of the most regular of regular verbs. Everyone
has been told that he never left the environs of his native
city, but it is not so easy to explain the thoughts he had
which made scholars from all over Europe come to Königsberg to hear him lecture and to participate in the table-talk
that made him known as one of the great conversationalists
in that age of great talkers.

Perhaps the only real excitement in his otherwise quiet
life was provided by the royal prohibition on his teaching and
writing on the subject of religion. This ban of censorship
was applied soon after his chief work on religion was published, though he had been having trouble with the censor
during its publication and had had to employ somewhat
roundabout procedures to have it published. Kant's response
to the ban was: "As your Majesty's humble servant, I agree
not to publish or teach on religious subjects." But when
Friedrich Wilhelm II died, Kant again felt free to publish
his thoughts on religion, explaining then the mental reserva-
tion which lay hidden in the form of his obedience to the
royal censor. That is, he was bound as the servant of Friedrich Wilhelm II to do what was required, but he was not
bound in this way to that king's successors. To this clever
ruse we owe the later editions of one of the most important
religious treaties of the eighteenth century, *Religion within
the Limits of Reason Alone.*

Before we take up this work, however, we must trace the
path along which Kant gradually approached it. His most
important book was the *Critique of Pure Reason,* published
in 1781. This vast and difficult masterpiece of philosophy had
as one of its purposes to show that human knowledge is not
able to extend to things which cannot be experienced. In
this respect, Kant's conclusions are somewhat like those of
Hume, but they are reached by a very different route, and it

is, regrettably, difficult to follow closely what he called its "thorny paths." But the outcome, at least, is clear: metaphysics, or knowledge of utimate reality and a supersensuous world, is not possible; all our knowledge is restricted to the world of phenomena, or nature, which is only the appearance of an unknown reality; of this world, scientific knowledge is objectively valid.

Among the objects included in the traditional scope of metaphysics, of course, is God. In striking down metaphysics, Kant denies that we can have any knowledge of God. Philosophers who had believed that they could prove the existence of God had transgressed the limits Kant found in knowledge. But instead of just writing off these proofs as illegitimate because they belonged to metaphysics, Kant showed, by long and intricate arguments, that the proofs for the existence of God are fallacious.

There are three classical arguments for the existence of God, and Kant examines each. They are the ontological, the cosmological, and the teleological (or argument from design).

The ontological argument was invented by St. Anselm in the eleventh century, but was rejected by St. Thomas Aquinas. It was revived in the seventeenth century by Descartes and was used by Spinoza. It is meant to prove the existence of God from the definition of God as a perfect being. Any characteristic (predicate) which is implied by the definition of a thing must apply to it. A perfect being, the argument runs, must possess all perfections, for otherwise it would not be perfect. Existence is a perfection; therefore God exists. Just as "triangle that does not have three sides" is a self-contradictory concept, so also "nonexistent perfect being" is said to be self-contradictory.

Kant refutes this argument by showing that "exists" is not a predicate at all, and therefore it cannot be a predicate of a perfect being, even if a perfect being should in fact exist. Though in grammar the word "existent" is as good a predicate as the word "perfect" and each obeys all the grammatical rules for the use of adjectives, logically, from the standpoint of how these words behave in inference, they are quite different. When one says of something that it exists, one is not ascribing a property to it, as when he says it is blue or it is perfect; a concept of a nonexistent thing x contains all the predicates that the concept of an existing x contains, for "existence" is not a predicate contained in, and therefore to be proved by, a concept. Kant's demonstration of this is sound, but it is very complicated—Kant is never easy to read—so we shall present a modern version of the critique of the ontological argument which is simpler and easier to follow.

The question is: Is a judgment that asserts that something exists, e.g., "Cats exist," logically like one that ascribes a predicate to a thing, e.g., "Cats scratch"? If they are not logically as well as grammatically similar, then "exist" is not a predicate that can be found by analyzing another predicate, like "perfect." Take, says Professor Broad,[2] a true statement, "Cats scratch." We can reformulate this sentence, and we find that the person who makes it means one of the following:

(a_1) If there were any cats, they would scratch; or
(a_2) There are cats, and they do scratch.

Now, on the assumption that "exists" is a predicate like "scratches," let us translate the sentence "Cats exist." We get:

(b_1) If there were any cats, they would exist; or
(b_2) There are cats, and they do exist.

Now (b_1) is necessarily true whether there are cats or not, and it does not tell us that there are cats. And (b_2) tells us that there are cats, twice. But if a man says "Cats scratch" and "Cats exist," he is saying something which is instructive

—i.e., it gives us information—and which happens to be true but which *might* have been false. Yet if we think "Cats exist" is logically like "Cats scratch," i.e., if we think "exist" is a predicate like "scratch," we would really be saying something uninstructive (b_2) or something necessarily true whether there are cats or not (b_1).

We now apply this paradigm to the judgments "God is perfect" and "God exists." Translating as before:

(c_1) If there were a God, He would be perfect; or
(c_2) There is a God, and He is perfect.
(d_1) If there were a God, He would exist; or
(d_2) There is a God, and He exists.

But none of these proves that God does exist: (d_1) is a tautology and is true whether God exists or not; (d_2) merely tells us, twice, that God does exist. There is no way to go, logically, from (c_1) to (c_2) or from (c_1) to (d_2).

The error of the ontological argument, therefore, is as follows. If "exists" is a predicate, then all statements that a thing exists (like $[b_1]$, $[b_2]$, $[d_1]$ and $[d_2]$) are either logically necessary or uninstructive, merely repeating themselves. But this is not the kind of truth we mean when we say a thing exists. To find out whether a thing exists, we have to examine facts, not just do logic to find out if the statement that something exists is logically necessary like "*a* is *a*." Hence the ontological argument, since it implies a false conclusion about how we get knowledge of existing things, is invalid.

From the ontological argument, Kant passes on to the other two arguments which are allegedly based upon the facts of experience and not upon empty logic. The cosmological argument is one that argues from the existence of the world to the existence of a necessary being as its cause or condition. This is the familiar causal argument: Anything which exists has a cause, which has a cause, which has a cause . . .; there must be a cause of everything which is not an effect of anything else. This is the first cause, or God. Put another way: If things in the world are dependent for their existence on something else, and do exist, then there must be something that is not dependent on anything else for *its* existence. This would be a necessary being, or God.

The objection to this argument is that it would not, even if otherwise valid, lead to a conception of God. For "first cause" and "necessary being" are not equivalent to "God" unless "first cause" and "necessary being" are equivalent to "perfect being," and "perfect being" must imply "existing being." Hence, at a crucial stage in this argument, the ontological argument is surreptitiously introduced. It is one link in this chain, and when it breaks the whole falls to the ground.

The physico-teleological argument, as Kant calls the argument from design, is already familiar to us from Hume's discussion. "This proof," says Kant

deserves to be mentioned with respect. It is the oldest, the clearest, and the most accordant with the common reason of mankind. It enlivens the study of nature. . . . It suggests ends and purposes . . . and extends our knowledge of nature by means of the guiding concept of a special unity, the principle of which is outside nature.[3]

Through knowledge gained under the guidance of the principle that all the parts of nature are interconnected under law as if by a Divine Intelligence, the belief in a Supreme Author of Nature "acquires the force of an irresistible conviction."

Nevertheless, the argument is logically inadequate. It is easy to see that it is a special case of the argument from effect (nature) to cause (God), and because that cosmological argument depends upon the ontological argument if it is to prove the existence of God, the teleological argument likewise falls.

The conclusion of the *Critique of Pure Reason* is, therefore, that no theoretically valid arguments for the existence
of God can be given, because Kant thought that these were
the only three possible rational arguments. The *Critique of
Pure Reason* did not, however, deny the existence of God;
it only denied that we could know it. He said: "I have found
it necessary to deny *knowledge,* in order to make room for
faith."[4] This sounds a good bit like some passage already
quoted from Hume; Hume said that theology could not be
based upon reason, and that if we would be religious we
should have to have recourse to faith.

But though Hume and Kant sound as though they were
saying the same thing, in fact they were not. Hume contrasts *reason* with faith, and when he recommends faith he
knows that it will be taken with the proper grain of salt. Kant
contrasts faith with *knowledge,* not with *reason,* because he
believed that there was a reasonable form of faith, faith that
a rational man could not fail to have and remain rational in
tracing out the implications of his experience. Such faith is
rational but it is not knowledge; yet it is not a blind faith
that has no reasonal standards and criteria and that arises
only from our emotions and sentiments. When Kant makes
room for rational faith in his philosophy, it is without the
skeptical and perhaps ironic attitude with which Hume had
recommended faith just a few years earlier. Faith for Hume,
as for most theologians, is something outside the realm of
reason; faith for Kant is only one of the aspects of reason,
the other being knowledge.

Rational faith is based on morality, not on science and
speculative philosophy. We must therefore look briefly at
Kant's ethical theory as expounded in his second great work,
the *Critique of Practical Reason.* Kant made a sharp distinction between actions which are moral and those which
are merely proper or prudent. A prudent action, like telling
the truth in order not to lose one's good standing, is one that

is likely to be successful in achieving some purpose or satisfying some desire we have. The desire may be selfish or unselfish; but so long as we do the action solely because we want to accomplish some end we desire, the action is merely prudent; it may not be morally wrong, but it is not a genuinely moral action, done because it is morally right. A moral action is one which has a unique motive, the motive of doing the right action because it is right, and it is one we ought to do regardless of any desires which may have to be frustrated by it. Reason, operating on our desires, may lead to prudent or clever actions; but pure reason itself, acknowledging a moral law which is not a law of how to satisfy our desires or to be happy, provides the motive for genuine morality.

The question is: Why are we motivated by our reason's acknowledgment of the moral law? Some would say it is because reason recognizes the moral law as a law given by God, who will reward us for our obedience. But Kant did not say this, for this would obliterate the distinction between morality and prudence. It would make Christianity only the most enlightened form of selfishness, with eternal rewards in the hereafter outweighing the advantages which might accrue to us in our earthly life if we were immoral but careful. In such a conception as this, there is no more moral worth in obeying God, whom we do not see, than in obeying a traffic policeman, whom we do see.

Kant said that we respect the moral law because it is a law which we, as reasonable beings, legislate for ourselves. We are not merely subjects in the realm of the moral law; we are also sovereigns and legislators. In his political theory, he held that men could not be legitimately bound to laws imposed upon them by fear of the power of the state; such laws make men slaves, not citizens. Laws are valid only to the extent that we participate in their establishment and thereby give free consent to them. Analogously, he said that the moral law binds us only by virtue of our free consent which is shown in our participation in its establishment.

Reason does not so much discover the moral law as decree it. The moral law is not only a law for reasonable beings, but a law reasonable beings give to themselves and voluntarily undertake to obey. Kant calls this the concept of moral autonomy, or moral freedom from all laws which do not have their origin in our own reason.

It is no accident that Kant was a follower of Rousseau and believed in self-government by the people. He extended this concept, however, far beyond the political sphere and regarded the moral law as a law given by ourselves and to ourselves. The concept of God as the source of moral law is replaced by the concept of ourselves as free rational beings, both sovereign and subject in the kingdom of morality.

It looks as though Kant has firmly banished the notion of God from any place in his ethical theory. Certainly he has built a moral theory that is not based upon any knowledge of God, indeed one that is not built even upon faith in God. Yet the stone that has been thrown out of the foundations is given an essential place in the superstructure. Let us then see how Kant went about to re-establish and rehabilitate the concept of God.

Morality, as we have seen, cannot be based upon the desire for happiness; that desire, plus intelligence, makes only for prudence and propriety; and it may lead actually to immorality. But Kant knew that we cannot give up our desire for happiness, however able we may become to control it and to disregard its enticements when we are trying to do our duty. Nor should we give it up, but only control it so that it does not infect our consciousness of duty and prevent us from being willing to do what duty requires of us. In fact, it is inconceivable that in a rational world, moral values should be permanently out of concord with our other legitimate values and inescapable desires, as they often seem to be in this vale of tears. The highest good in the world is not stark virtue, but happiness proportional to and dependent upon virtue. Virtue is not happiness, but it is worthiness to be happy; and if the world is rational at all, we cannot think of this worthiness to be happy as inevitably and invariably frustrated. We know that in the world as we experience it, the proportion between virtue and happiness does not often exist; the morally best people are not always the happiest. We do not know that this proportion is made actual in another world beyond this, though religion teaches that it is. We cannot know this, not because it is false but because we have no knowledge at all of what lies beyond our experience.

But unless we are to regard the moral law as null and void, i.e., as not logically consistent in the order it requires us to enforce upon our will and desires, we must at least believe that this proportioning of desert and reward is possible in the world which we do not know, in the world of things as they are instead of as they appear to our senses. The moral law requires us to seek the highest good, and if we are not to give up the moral law as chimerical, we must believe that what it holds before us as a moral ideal must be at least possible. The highest good is possible, however, only if God exists as the moral governor of the universe, dispensing reward and punishment according to our moral deserts. Hence Kant concluded that God is a postulate, logically required by our acknowledgment of the full implications of the moral law, which we cannot deny.

God, then, is not an object of knowledge but of faith, and of a rational faith and not of a faith based upon sentiment. Is this sufficient to give stability to the moral sentiment? Or must my knowledge of what I ought to do be based upon knowledge of God? Kant answers: Faith is sufficient; and such knowledge would be dangerous to morality. If we knew that God existed, transgression of the law would indeed be shunned, and the commanded would be performed. But because the disposition from which actions should be done cannot be instilled by any command, and because the spur to action would in this case be always present and external, reason would have no need to endeavor to gather its strength to resist the inclinations by a vivid idea of the dignity of the law. Thus most actions conforming to the law would be done from fear, few would be done from hope, none from duty.[5]

It was therefore for the sake of morality that Kant denied knowledge in order to make room for faith. The faith he provided a place for was not faith in contrast to reason, but faith as an adjunct to moral reason. It is rational, but it is not knowledge.

It is not even a substitute for knowledge. We do not go a certain distance toward God, as it were, along the path of knowledge, and then finish the journey by an act of faith, as in the philosophy of St. Thomas. The whole movement of the mind toward God is from the beginning a morally motivated movement, not scientifically motivated or guided. The resulting conception of God is a wholly ethical one. The only valid theology is ethico-theology, and all the attributes we properly ascribe to God are either moral (holiness, beneficence, justice) or are derived from them. This conception, Kant argues, is less anthropomorphic than that of those who use the argument from design, for we have a purely rational conception of moral attributes, independent of their embodiment in human form.

Holding this rational faith in God is the same thing as having true religion. "Religion," he says, "is the recognition of all duties as divine commands. . . ."[6] It is not that they *are* divine commands, or that they owe their authority over us to their being decrees of a divine lawgiver who also created us; for in that event, we should have to know about God before we could know what our duty is, and we do not know

God, while even the most unphilosophical person knows his duty. Moreover, such a theory would be incompatible with moral self-government, or autonomy. Religion is not the basis for morality, but rather the contrary; religion is a rational attitude based upon morality, tracing out its ramifications in our conception of the world we do not know. From this, it follows that there are no specifically religious duties; there is no duty, for instance, to believe in the existence of God. Morality and religion differ from each other in their formal structure and vocabulary, but not in their substance. Any religion that requires anything of man other than earnest and conscientious morality is mere superstition and idolatry.

Christianity, even in its historically imperfect form, according to Kant approaches the ideal of a pure moral theology more closely than any other religion. The doctrine of Christianity presents the highest moral insights in symbolic language, which we must be careful to interpret properly. For instance, the essence of both morality and religion is destroyed if our reason for obedience to the moral law is a hope of reward in heaven. Moral philosophy requires that we act out of respect for law itself, while religion requires that the motive for genuine goodness be love of God in purity of heart; but to love God means to do willingly His commandments. The duty and the goodness are the same in any specific case. One of Kant's pupils wrote him: "I verily believe that if Jesus could have heard your lectures on the moral law, He would have said, 'That is what I meant by the love of God.'" Such adulation was alien to Kant's dry unenthusiasm; but the influence of moralistic Pietism persisted throughout his ethical writings, even when he was most adamant in refusing to base ethics on a prior religious belief.

Five years after the *Critique of Practical Reason*, Kant published his *Religion within the Limits of Reason Alone*, the book that brought him under the censure of the Prussian government for having "misused his philosophy to the detriment and disparagement of many fundamental tenets of Holy Scripture and Christianity." It is hard to forgive the bigoted royal censor; yet it is not difficult to see what it was in this book that was offensive to him.

The principal themes of this book, in so far as they bear upon religious disputes and the authority of the church, are Kant's theory of the natural evolution of religion and his distinction between service and pseudo-service of God, which he defines as the conflict between true religion and clericalism. There is also, in this book, a new argument for the rationality of faith in God.

Kant held that there is an evolutionary progress in morality from a state of nature, in which there is war of each against all, through civil society in which men are held together in uneasy peace through the externally imposed decrees of a powerful ruler, to an ethical commonwealth, or a community in which men hold themselves together by their reverence for law and by trying to treat each other as ends in themselves. Moral law is then regarded as if it were a divine command, and the ethical commonwealth is a people united by common allegiance to a supposed author of these commands, namely God. The ethical commonwealth is, therefore, the Kingdom of God or the Church Invisible.

Human nature, being imperfect, and human beings, having an innate propensity to evil, are such that perfect virtue is unattainable. "Out of such crooked lumber as man is made of," he says elsewhere, "nothing perfectly straight can be built." Perfect virtue is hardly even an effective ideal for men who are aware of the forces of evil in themselves, of their weakness against them, and of the evil in others who surround them. Virtue is an inward state, though it can be securely achieved only in a social situation in which others are likewise committed to its attainment; but no one is responsible for the moral state of society. But just as he held, in the second *Critique*, that what we must believe in order to be moral we have a right to believe and indeed must believe in order to organize our moral conceptions in a rational way, here he repeats this kind of argument for a somewhat different conception of God. He argues that the moral need for the ethical commonwealth, which man alone cannot satisfy, requires us to have faith in God, not as the rewarder and punisher, but as the author of the moral system in which men can indeed do their duty. This is faith not merely in God, but faith in the establishment of the Kingdom of God as a condition for the realization of our whole duty.[7]

In fact, however, the visible church appears on the scene of history long before the Church Invisible makes itself effective in the consciences of good men working together for moral betterment. It always begins with some alleged revelation, and its dogma is always worked out with priestly meticulousness and appears as ritual. The visible church, morever, is often only a political power, with the vested interests of the priestly caste often allying themselves with the powerful of this earth. The visible church, therefore, is often the enemy of true virtue, for it locates the source of the moral law in Scripture (which, as Spinoza and Kant together point out, it often misreads) instead of in man's sovereign moral reason. Only later does there begin an ethical and rational critique of ecclesiastical and dogmatic faith, to the end that the church, originally only an institution in the power-structure of society, is refined into the invisible moral commonwealth. Ecclesiastical faith—faith in Scripture, faith in clerical authority, faith leading to outward conformity in hope of an eternal reward—is replaced or gradually reformed into pure rational faith in God and His Kingdom, the faith of the uncoerced moral consciousness.

In step with this slow evolution, the pseudo-service of

God in a statutory or clericalistic church is gradually replaced by the legitimate service of God: "Whatever, over and above good life-conduct, man fancies that he can do to become well-pleasing to God is mere religious illusion and the pseudo-service of God."[8] For example, Kant believed that prayer was not only ineffectual in changing the way of the world but morally dangerous to him who prays, because it permits him to believe that there is a lenient Governor of the universe who may interfere with nature and history for his benefit, provided only He is approached with proper ceremonies and feelings. This makes us think that ritual propitiation is the proper service of God, rather than conscientious obedience to moral law. This false conception of God degrades the rational conception of God into something anthropomorphic and exposes religion to contempt; at the same time it leads men away from true morality by minimizing the inexorableness of moral law, whose demands are not to be abrogated by piety in desperation.

Men should free themselves, so far as possible, from the slave mentality, which thinks of God as an arbitrary monarch whose favor can be won by ritual and ceremonial orthodoxy or asceticism. This emancipation means replacing a religious ethics with an ethical religion, the substitution of actions done because our conscience or reason tells us they are right for actions done with an eye to divine rewards. The former actions are accompanied, however, by the faith that there is in the universe some Being who helps us to do what we know we ought to do, and who will in fact reward us for doing so.

This last great transition can occur only if men are allowed the freedom to think openly on religious questions. That such freedom of thought and of the press is essential for ethical and religious improvement, indeed for the welfare of the state itself, was forcefully argued in 1785 in Kant's little essay, *What is Enlightenment?* This essay insisted that

a teacher or clergyman, though an agent of the state or
church, does not act contrary to duty when he brings his
critical thoughts to the attention of the learned public, even
if his official duties require him to teach what he is told to
teach although he may not wholly subscribe to the letter
of the teaching. "But as a scholar," Kant said, the teacher or
preacher ". . . has complete freedom, even the calling, to
communicate to the public all his carefully tested and well-
meaning thoughts on that which is erroneous in the symbol
[i.e., in the visible form of the church] and to make sugges-
tions for the better organization of the religious body and
church. In doing this, there is nothing that could be laid
as a burden on his conscience."[9] If, however, he is so opposed to the spirit of the teaching that his public utterances
as a minister are only hypocritical, he should resign his
office, but the state should continue to allow him to write
as he thinks.

Regrettably, the Prussian censor did not agree with this,
and the Sage of Königsberg was forbidden to lay his thoughts
before the learned world, even in books which few could
understand. And the irony of it all is that, as Spinoza saw,
the attempt to chain thought was bound to fail; and Kant's
thoughts live on, while even the name of the censor is almost
forgotten.

SUGGESTED READING

Most of Kant's writings on religion which have been translated into English can be got in inexpensive editions, and
these are cited in the notes. The long introductions by Theo-
dore M. Greene and John R. Silber to the *Religion within the
Limits of Reason Alone* (Harper Torchbook, 1960) are especially recommended.

The best brief introduction to Kant as a whole is perhaps
S. Körner's *Kant* (London: Penguin Books, 1955), but

Körner pays little attention to Kant's views on religion. More adequate in this context is A. D. Lindsay's *Kant* (London: Benn, 1934). C. C. J. Webb's *Kant's Philosophy of Religion* (Oxford: Clarendon, 1926) and F. E. England's *Kant's Conception of God* (London: Allen and Unwin, 1929) are standard and valuable, but dull. I have given a detailed examination of Kant's "moral argument" for the existence of God in my *Commentary on Kant's Critique of Practical Reason* (Chicago: University of Chicago Press, 1960), Chapters XIII and XIV. Especially interesting and controversial is the little book by Richard Kroner, *Kant's Weltanschauung*, translated by John E. Smith (Chicago: University of Chicago Press, 1956).

VI

Nietzsche

I am no man, I am dynamite." Thus spake
Nietzsche.

Friedrich Nietzsche, who lived from 1844 to 1900, is the
hardest to understand in our group of philosophers because
he is the easiest to misunderstand. Yet he is the easiest to
read: his epigrams, his vivid symbols, his bombast, his
powerful poems and prose-poems make reading him an unforgettable experience. Unforgettable, but not easily diges-
tible. The reader must supply his own framework for
interpreting the manifold of *aperçus* which was Nietzsche, or
he must borrow one from some commentator. Nietzsche was
like St. Paul, says George Morgan, in being "all things to
all men," and the reader can take his pick from commentators
who see Nietzsche as a proto-Nazi or a crypto-Christian, as
a nihilist or decadent, as a Darwinian or anti-Darwinian,
as "gentle Nietzsche" or "brutal Nietzsche," as "wise
Nietzsche" or "mad Nietzsche." The tragic fact that Nietzsche became insane has been used as a convenient expedient for playing down the parts of his work that a reader,
convinced of his own sanity, finds repulsive.

The fundamental conceptions of his philosophy, as I see
them, are: the innocence of existence, and the will to power.

By the innocence of existence is meant the doctrine that
all our moral categories, such as good and duty, are inven-
tions, human all-too-human. They are not concepts describing what there is there in the world, but they express, rather,

a tacit condemnation of the world. Nietzsche called himself an "immoralist." He meant that his conception of the world was not infected with moral prejudice. He thought he saw the prime facts which underlay all moral judgment, and that they showed that moral judgment was illegitimate and impudent. Just as we have caffeine-free coffee and nicotine-free cigarettes, Nietzsche claimed that in him we have a "moraline-free philosophy," one which is not poisoned by "moralic acid." Immoralism does not mean that the world is morally bad just because it is said not to be morally good; it means that the world is alien to our conceptions of good and evil. It is "beyond good and evil." Moral judgment is a distortion of fact. Making moral judgments is a natural phenomenon that arises late in evolution, and it is one that is necessary for self-discipline and for all cultural accomplishment. But it is a phenomenon that can be explained without supposing that good and evil are objective powers in the world, and we can grow beyond it by achieving a kind of second innocence, a rebirth which is symbolized by the child, whose world-view is not yet tainted and warped by moralistic culture:

[The spirit of man] once loved "thou shalt" as most sacred: now he must find illusion and caprice even in the most sacred, that freedom from his love may become his prey: a lion [a destroyer] is needed for such prey.

But say, my brothers, what can the child do that even the lion could not do? . . . The child is innocence and forgetting, a new beginning, a game, a self-propelled wheel, a first movement, a sacred "Yes." For the game of creation, . . . a sacred "yes" is needed. . . .[1]

Nietzsche's philosophy of immoralism, he thought, was a necessary precondition for the creation of new values, values consonant with reality instead of vain protests against the real in the name of some spurious ideal. The old tables of the law had to be broken so that new tables with new values could be set up. A new innocence was called for, a rejection of our sophisticated culture which hides the facts under nice words and condemns reality in the name of unreal values.

The second basic conception is that of the will to power. Many horrendous meanings have been read into this concept; fascistic and Freudian meanings have been found prefigured in it. We must concede that Nietzsche did not make its meaning perfectly clear. But it was a conception that had a quite long and respectable philosophical tradition behind it; something comparable to it was in Spinoza and Schopenhauer, and something similar to it appeared later in the philosophy of Bergson.

The will to power, like the analogous concepts in these other philosophers, was not exclusively a psychological notion. Nietzsche used it as the name for the ultimate energy or force; indeed, it named the ultimate reality itself, which for Nietzsche was action, doing, happening, not dead stuff or lifeless matter. Its workings in man, of course, are where it is most readily seen, but here its workings are often disguised so that they seem to be the very opposite of a will to power. Gentle people were as shocked to hear that the driving force of their most generous aspirations was will to power as they were a few years later to hear from Freud that it was libido. One thing the will to power is not, though it has it as one of its manifestations: it is not just naked, brutal drive to destruction. The will to power is shown as well in asceticism as in meticulous self-care, in self-discipline and the timidities of conventional morality as in Dionysian frenzy. It is shown in Napoleon's ambitions for conquest and in Charles V's renunciation of political power and retreat to a monastery, in Mozart as in Richard Wagner. Knowledge itself is will to power, perhaps its highest form; there is no "immaculate perception" or knowledge divorced from the effort to enhance power.

But how does one thing appear in so many antithetical

forms? How can it be the same will to power which shows itself in the euphoria of drunkenness and in saintly asceticism? Nietzsche answered: The will to power may work through *resentment* as well as through a direct and dynamic push in a straight line to its goal. When a person's freedom of action over nature and others is thwarted, the will to power does not cease to be active. It makes a detour; it gets to its goal indirectly. This detour is the path of resentment. The resentment need not be conscious; it usually is not recognized for what it is. Morality is the chief form of this resentment. The weak resent the power of the strong and condemn it morally; they feel that they are motivated in other ways, and hence are good. But Nietzsche said of them: "Verily, I have often laughed at the weaklings who thought themselves good because they had no claws."[2]

Because the will to power may act directly, or indirectly through resentment, there arise two antithetical conceptions of worth and value. Those who are able to exercise the will to power directly approve of the traits found in the strong and aristocratic, in the fearless rulers of men. They acclaim action, spontaneity, individuality, independence, domination, creativity, pride, the cruelty and magnanimous grace of the conqueror to the conquered. These traits and acts they call "good." The traits of those whom they dominate they call "bad," where "bad" indicates that they are held in contempt and are despised. They are the mean and common traits. The contemptible traits include patience, piety, pity, niggardly self-denial, and a Uriah Heep type of humility— in fact, all so-called virtues in so far as they grow from an awareness of impotence and not from self-disciplined strength and self-respect. Pratings about the equality and rights of man are the self-protective devices of the members of the herd, "the many-too-many" who cannot stand alone, but whose "love" for each other is only a mask for their fear of their betters.

Exactly the same will to power in the weak and oppressed takes the form of resentment at the free-wheeling, yea-saying, joyous life of their oppressors. The oppressed call their own traits of patience, pity, and long-suffering "good," and they think that they are denials of the will to power, which they consider evil and believe to be present only in their hated superiors. They call the traits of their masters "evil" because they think these hated and feared traits manifest a will to power which is not only inimical to the decent common man but wholly foreign to his nature.

The traits developed in each class are inevitable. They define the character and personality which is valued by each caste. The moral valuations put upon them are likewise inevitable; it is inevitable that the weak shall esteem pity and that the strong shall esteem hardness and discipline. The moral values of the lower caste, which condemn the direct, natural, and vital characters of their rulers, destroy the conception of the innocence of existence. That which is natural—i.e., the headlong activity of the strong—is condemned, and nature herself (now called "lower nature" or "animal nature") is considered evil. Nature is morally condemned, and men then try to make themselves independent of her or superior to her by ascetic practices and otherworldly concern.

Now there occurred, according to Nietzsche, the most momentous event in all history. He called it the "slaves' revolt in morals," but it is otherwise known as the birth of Judaism.

The slaves' revolt in morals begins with this, that *ressentiment* itself becomes creative and gives birth to values: the *ressentiment* of those who are denied the real reaction, that of the deed, and who compensate with an imaginary revenge.[3]

They take this revenge on those who do have the outlet in action and deed. It was a successful "revolt of the bungled

and botched"[4] against the naturally superior. The lower
caste succeeded in fastening its own conception of the good
upon the master class, and thus occurred the first transvaluation of values: the lower virtues became the higher, and
the higher, lower. What had been thought of as bad is now
seen as good, and what had been noble and great is called
evil. The first shall be last, and the last first; he who would
be master must become the servant of all, and so on. When
this transvaluation occurred, the spirit of the superior was
corrupted. His natural power was thwarted by foisting upon
him an illusory consciousness of a debt to some higher
power which was represented as a vengeful god standing on
the side of the lowly and humble and poor in spirit. Nature
was condemned as original sin, and the terrible disease of a
bad conscience for being natural infected the innocent.

The fantasy of a better world than this, of a world in
which the ideals of the herd are realized, of a world of rewards for lower-caste weaknesses and punishments for upper-
caste strengths, was established as an eternal reality, standing
over against the mundane reality we know, as a condemnation of it and a consolation for its melancholy. Neighbor-love
among the many-too-many destroyed love of the best, which
is hard and stern; pity strengthened the mutual-aid society
of the weak. The weakest members of our race were preserved; the race itself was weakened. The priesthood of
defamers of this world and prophets of another won the
power, and they have enjoyed it ever since. They preached
asceticism against innocent joy in existence and action; they
substituted blind faith for courageous reason; they hid the
truth because they could not stand it; they later substituted
Christian faith for works as the way to the higher world. To
be sure, the priests did an essential job: they helped tame
men and bring them discipline, but they overtamed them.
They made men hate themselves. When this terrible stage
of alienation from existence is reached, there is what Nie-

tzsche called nihilism: the utter devaluation of existence, the feeling that *nothing* is worthwhile. This strangles all creative power, which depends upon taking a passionate stand for the values of existence; it was for writing *Parsifal* that Nietzsche condemned his former hero Richard Wagner. The church brought about this nihilism as a matter of principle, and in the name of an ideal:

> . . . to shatter the strong, to spoil great hopes, to cast suspicion on the delight in beauty, to break down everything autonomous, manly, conquering, and imperious—all instincts which are natural to the highest and most successful type of "man"—into uncertainty, distress of conscience, and self-destruction; forsooth, to invert all love of the earthly and of supremacy over the earth, into hatred of the earth and earthly things—*that* is the task the Church imposed on itself. . . .[5]

This game of the priests—a deadly, world-historical game, be it said—was almost up, Nietzsche thought. He said that Europe had outgrown "the Christian fable," and had done so because there is a seed of self-destruction in its teachings. This seed is the ascetic ideal of the love of truth. Not that the love of truth is characteristically Christian; but it comes about, as a kind of vocational or occupational virtue, in men who are given to the study of documents, the codification of traditions, the systematization of ideas. At first, this virtue is exercised within narrow limits, and is always circumscribed by a defensiveness against criticism of the truth of the doctrine *as a whole,* but it is at work within the confines of the doctrine, and men's intellects and indeed their love of truth were sharpened in centuries of dialectic, definition, and heresy-hunting. Then this love of truth gets out of hand, and discovers in its own secularization the real truth: atheism. Atheism is the final phase in the religious evolution of a will to power which has placed a value on honesty and truth. Atheism is "the awe-inspiring *catastrophe* of a two-thousand-year training in truth, which finally forbids itself *the lie of the belief in God*."[6] This paradox had not yet been recognized by the priests, though the growth of secularism based on science and objective history made them realize that their power was waning.

Zarathustra the Godless wandered down from his mountain and met a saint in the forest:

"And what is the saint doing in the forest?" asked Zarathustra.

The saint answered: "I make songs and sing them; and when I make songs, I laugh, cry, and hum: thus I praise God. With singing, crying, laughing, and humming, I praise the god who is my god. But what do you bring us as a gift?"

When Zarathustra had heard these words he bade the saint farewell and said: "What could I have to give you? But let me go quickly lest I take something from you!" And thus they separated, the old one and the man, laughing as two boys laugh.

But when Zarathustra was alone he spoke thus to his heart: "Could it be possible? This old saint in the forest has not yet heard anything of this, that *God is dead!*"[7]

You will have noticed that I spoke of the slave revolt in morals as the birth of Judaism, and then went directly to Nietzsche's condemnation of the Christian Church. But how did Christianity get into this history? Niezsche's answer was simple and direct: the Church is Jewish in reality, Christian only in name. "There was only *one* Christian, and he died on the cross."[8] "The Church is precisely the thing against which Jesus inveighed"; "What did Christ deny? Everything which today is called Christian."[9]

What we today call Christianity is morally and culturally a degradation of Judaism, not a reaction against it, least of all a correction to it. The decline from Judaism to Christianity, Nietzsche thought, is shown in the difference, an aesthetic as well as a moral difference, between the Old Testament and the New. In the former, there are "great men, an heroic landscape, and . . . the incomparable naïveté *of the strong heart*"; in the latter, "pure rococo of the soul, twisting angles and fancy touches, . . . [and] an occasional whiff of bucolic sweetness";[10] and the dishonesty of the Christian conception of the relation between them is nowhere better shown than in the fact that the Christians claimed the Old Testament to be a prelude to the New, and in doing so had to distort it into such a shape that the latter could be made to appear as the completion of the former, with every possible passage twisted into a "prophecy" of the events recounted in the New Testament. The Church is the product of this priestly deception, with neither the prophetic dignity and sublimity of the Old Testament nor the purity of Christ; it was the creation of St. Paul, a "genius in hatred," not of Jesus, who not only preached but practiced purity of heart and love.

Who was Jesus? According to Nietzsche, he was an unrealistic hater of reality, "seized with a longing for death," a visionary; after Nietzsche had read Dostoevski's novel by that name, he called Jesus "an Idiot." Jesus wanted to initiate a "Buddhistic peace-movement" in Judaism by stamping out resentment in favor of love. His doctrine of love for one's enemies; his doctrine that the Kingdom of God is in us and not of this world; his doctrine that all men and not merely the "chosen people" are the children of God—all these doctrines were so opposed to the Jewish ideology that the Jews had to kill him to remove a danger to themselves. Had he lived longer, Nietzsche sanctimoniously said, Jesus would have learned better and disavowed his own teaching: "Noble enough was he to recant."[11]

His disciples and, a little later, St. Paul made Christ into a hero for the Jews. This they did by preaching his second coming, which ushers in a new age for the Jews. They promised salvation and freedom to the depressed masses in Rome through the myth of his atonement for their sins and God's punishment of the pagans. Through him, the Jews

indeed did conquer Rome, which they could never have done
without him. Paul built his distorted figure of Christ into the
whole apparatus of a church, a thoroughly Jewish and unchristian institution; he and the later Church Fathers made
the little band of primitive Christians into the Church mili-
tant and, later, into the Church state. It was this institution,
with its holy hatreds, its sacred dogmas, its curses and de-
nunciations, which finally triumphed over Roman persecution. It triumphed over Rome and the northern barbarians,
only to become Romanized and barbarized itself; in this, the
Church finally triumphed over Christianity itself. In it the
slave revolt in morals reached its highest and most complete
and lasting form, and Nietzsche thundered his denunciation
like a prophet of old denouncing the enemies of Jehovah:

> I *condemn* Christianity. I raise against the Christian church
> the most terrible of all accusations that any accuser ever uttered.
> It is to me the highest of all conceivable corruptions. It has had
> the will to the last corruption that is even possible. The Christian
> church has left nothing untouched by its corruption; it has
> turned every value into an un-value, every truth into a lie, every
> integrity into a vileness of the soul. . . . I call it the one im-
> mortal blemish of mankind.[12]

The decline of the Church into nihilism was what he
exulted over. In the twilight of the Christian idols, he believed that the main factor in European culture of the past
had finally become impotent. That is why he said, "God is
dead," not "There is no God."

What was there to take the place of God, belief in Whom,
after all, had had some disciplining effect upon men? With
the death of God, Nietzsche believed that there was a chance
for the re-establishment of the consciousness of the innocence
of existence. There would be another transvaluation of values.
He made Zarathustra its prophet, Zarathustra being a metaphorical reincarnation of Zoroaster, who, he said, had first

introduced the illusion of moral good and evil into the world
and who should now be the mouthpiece of the movement to
drive it out again. Zarathustra is the John the Baptist for
the Superman, a being beyond good and evil, who would
have new values as direct manifestations of the will to power,
not as resentful expressions of it directed against existence
itself. The Superman would be the creator of new tables of
the law, preaching and practicing many Christian virtues
as overflowings of his bounteous creative nature, not as
denials of existence or as resentful actions squeezed from
one's own nature by frustrations. Of course he would have
also other virtues, which Christianity condemns as evil; chief
among them would be pride, hardness, and love of the here
and now.

Nietzsche's Superman is not a science-fiction hero; he is
not a being to be produced by eugenics and the Darwinian
struggle for existence, at some future time. He is rather
your "true self [which] does not lie deeply concealed within
you but immeasurably high above you."[13] The ethical im-
perative of the Superman is: *Become what thou art!* He is
the higher man who has overcome himself through discipline,
hardness, and the searing honesty of self-knowledge. He
alone of all men can bear the full truth about himself.

The Superman would be so yea-saying to existence that
he would embrace the most mysterious and mystical and
difficult of all of Nietzsche's teachings, that of the eternal
recurrence of all things. According to this, all actions are
repeated an infinite number of times in an infinite series
of world-cycles; the suffering as well as the joy of life will
recur endlessly. One who can say Yea to this, without feeling
that it is a tale told by an idiot, full of sound and fury
signifying nothing, has reaffirmed in the highest degree the
innocence of existence; he even says Yea to the historical
denials of the innocence of existence, to his own condemnation. He does not need the fiction of progress, because he

finds every moment of life worthy of such affirmation that he can will that it recur eternally. Mephistopheles' challenge to Faust—that Mephistopheles can produce one moment to which Faust, eternally dissatisfied, will exclaim, "Stay, thou art so beautiful!"—is victoriously met at every moment by the Superman. Least of all does the Superman need another world of changeless perfection (heaven) as a counterbalance to the transitoriness of the few good moments of our ordinary mundane existence. He brings this transitoriness itself as close as possible to the state of eternal existence by willing its infinite repetition, by saying to all passing events, "Yet once more!"

> O man, take care!
> What does the deep midnight declare?
> "I was asleep—
> From a deep dream I woke and swear:
> The world is deep,
> Deeper than day had been aware.
> Deep is its woe;
> Joy—deeper yet than agony:
> Woe implores: Go!
> But all joy wants eternity—
> Wants deep, wants deep eternity."[14]

SUGGESTED READINGS

The best inexpensive collection of Nietzsche's writings in English is *The Portable Nietzsche*, translated and edited by Walter Kaufmann (New York: The Viking Press, 1954; available also in paperback edition). Less dependable, but useful for including some works not in Kaufmann's selection, is *The Philosophy of Nietzsche*, translated by Thomas Common, *et al.* (New York: Random House—Modern Library, 1937). The translations in the latter volume are taken from *The Complete Works of Friedrich Nietzsche* (New York: The Macmillan Co., 1924). The reader of *The Will to Power* in Volumes XIV and XV of this edition should be warned that recent research has shown that much of this work is spurious. The introduction to Kaufmann's *The Portable Nietzsche* is very instructive; that to the Modern Library edition is poor and undependable.

The best studies of Nietzsche in English are by Kaufmann (*Nietzsche: Philosopher, Psychologist, Antichrist* [Princeton: Princeton University Press, 1950; available also in paperback edition]) and by George A. Morgan (*What Nietzsche Means* [Cambridge: Harvard University Press, 1941]).

VII

James

America's most important contribution to philosophy is Pragmatism. As an active movement in philosophy, it has lived out its time; but the good it did lives after it, and there is a strong pragmatistic element remaining in almost all American and British philosophers of today.

The pragmatistic movement was not something absolutely new with James and his friends back in the nineties; James called pragmatism simply "a new name for some old ways of thinking." These old ways of thinking can easily be found in earlier philosophers, such as Hobbes and Hume and even Kant. But for a philosophical system to have life outside the study of the philosopher, it must be responsive to the broader intellectual and cultural needs of its time and place. Pragmatism was a philosophy particularly appropriate to the venturesomeness, the unfinishedness, of American life, when Americans wanted a philosophy that would find activity, development, doing something in the here and now, in the center of experience where we Americans usually do put it. Something of the briskness and brashness of American life, which drove Henry James to England, was built into philosophy by his brother William (1842-1910).

James classified thinkers into two groups: the tough-minded and the tender-minded. The tender-minded were those who liked to think and feel the oneness of things, who liked ideals and high abstractions, and who were contemptuous of nasty little facts that threatened their dreams. The tough-minded were more realistic, more ready to live with probabilities, more willing to take things on the go and to work patiently for better things, instead of feeling that really all things were good in a perfect universe in which nothing could be changed. Spinoza, for example, was tender-minded and Hume was tough-minded by this criterion. We find in James a very singular mixture of tender-mindedness and tough-mindedness, though he liked to think of himself as tough-minded.

We find in James, accordingly, two somewhat different attitudes towards religion. He was always a secular philosopher by the criterion we have adopted, but he was sometimes secular in one way and sometimes in another. The two kinds of religious philosophy that he developed are not incompatible with each other; but they also are not very close to each other. I shall call them his pragmatism and, for lack of a better word, his spiritualistic pluralism.

Let us first consider James's pragmatism in general before we see how he applied it to religion. For pragmatists, truth is something that happens to an idea. An idea is true if it works. This does not mean that it is true if it can be used for making money, or if believing it just gives us a good feeling inside. An idea works if it does what an idea is supposed to do, and that is to make a difference in our experience, a difference of the kind anticipated in or promised by the idea. James said, in a metaphor that was almost viciously misunderstood at the time, that truth is the "cash value" of an idea. By this he meant to compare an idea to a check. A beautiful check may bounce; you cannot see whether it is a good check by examining it or by knowing where it came from. To find out if it is good, you take it to a bank to see if you can get cash for it. It is worth only as much as the cash it procures for you. Similarly, an idea is a draft on future experience, which the future experience may or may not honor. Experience honors an idea, i.e., shows it to be true, if the experience turns out to be as the idea promised. True ideas are those which guide our experience to an anticipated destination; false ideas are those which lead us to experiences which disappoint the expectation we had in holding the idea; empty ideas are those which do not lead anywhere, which do not prepare us for one thing rather than its opposite.

An idea is a hypothesis to be tested in future experience, not something to be cherished for its own sake alone. A hypothesis is a plan of action; the action can verify or refute the hypothesis. " 'The true' . . . is only the expedient in the way of our thinking, just as 'the right' is only the expedient in the way of our behaving"[1]—only we must take "expedient" to describe some long-term success, not something that just gets us out of a temporary scrape.

So much for the theory of knowledge of pragmatism. Many philosophers, such as the positivists described in Chapter I, have held this much of the theory of truth and have concluded: ideas about God are not subject to this empirical test; no future experience is predictably different if God does or does not exist; theological ideas are therefore, if not false, at least empty and meaningless. But James did not make this positivistic inference. He did not do so because he did not clearly distinguish between two different tests which may be involved here, and he attached equal weight to each, sometimes using one and sometimes the other.

The important distinction is between (a) the consequences for experience of the truth of an idea acted upon, and (b) the consequences for experience of believing in the truth of an idea.

This perhaps seems like an overly subtle distinction, but it is one that is so important that I shall try to make it clear by a simple illustration. Suppose I wish to go to Boston by train. I have an idea, that is, I believe, that a train leaves the station at noon. This idea has no consequences unless I act upon it. But the consequences may be of two kinds. There are first simply the consequences of believing it; these consequences are that I shall go to the station. The second are the consequences it has if I believe it *and* if it is in fact true. Consequences of this kind are that when I reach the station I shall hear the train announced and that if I take it I shall reach Boston; reaching Boston is what shows that my idea was true. In ordinary life, therefore, we distinguish between the consequences of believing a hypothesis, viz., going to the station, and the consequences of the truth of the hypothesis which is believed, viz., getting to Boston.

We shall now observe James in his efforts to apply the pragmatic test to the religious hypothesis. We must distinguish between the consequences in the world of discoverable and observable facts of the truth or falsity of the religious hypothesis, and the consequences in our lives of believing in this idea, *whether* it be true or false. In a religious context, we must distinguish, as it were, between going to church (like going to the station) and getting to heaven (like getting to Boston). James indicates that these two tests are involved by saying that the religious hypothesis itself has two parts. Religion says, according to James, first that "the best things are the more eternal things," and second that "we are better off even now" if we believe the first.

The existence of God is the usual way in which the religions of mankind, especially Christianity, have envisaged the eternity of the perfect; and faith is the usual form in which religions have found the workings of this hypothesis in our present life. There are other ways in which the religious hypothesis of the eternity of the good can be expressed, each with its specific nuances. I shall here be narrower than James was, for the sake of simplicity, and discuss in his terms only the hypothesis of the existence of God. This is not an hypothesis like that of the existence of atoms. We cannot devise an objective experiment which will turn out one way if God exists and another way if God does not exist. For this reason, the only test we can apply is a test of the consequences of accepting the belief, which will be the same in fact, so far as we can know, whether the belief is true or not. The belief or its rejection or merely a suspension of judgment about it will make a difference in someone's behavior and thereby indirectly in the go of other things in the world. In this event, James said, we have a right to consider the consequences of believing the idea when we cannot find a test for truth of the idea itself.

It is not just an excuse for wishful thinking that James was giving here. If we know whether an idea is true by virtue of having explored and checked its consequences, we have no right to disbelieve it however much we would like to reject it. If we have shown by its consequences that it is false, we have no right to believe in it because we like the emotional kick we get out of accepting it. No, the test James applied to beliefs which cannot be directly tested was restricted in four ways.

First, it is applicable only where knowledge based upon the idea itself in its implications for our experience of future facts is and will remain unavailable.

Second, it is legitimate to apply it only where a choice among alternative hypotheses (which James called an "option") is to be made among *live* hypotheses. Live hypotheses are those which have some appeal to us, hypotheses we could act upon; an option between becoming a Mohammedan or becoming a theosophist, he said, is not for us a live option, though it might be a live one for other people.

Third, the choice to be made in this way must be a momentous one. It must have consequences serious enough to engage us, not consequences that are trivial and, if we do not like them, easily avoided. Believing that an intimate friend is sincere or has betrayed my friendship is a moment-

ous option for me; believing that it will rain instead of
snowing is not likely to be a momentous option.

Fourth, the choice must be forced. I do not have to make
a choice between going out with my umbrella or without it,
for I can decide not to go out at all. But in matters which
are relevant here, I cannot suspend judgment: if I so much as
entertain the hypothesis that my friend has betrayed me, the
friendship is already lost. Similarly, not to believe in the
existence of God simply because we do not have sufficient
empirical proof of it, James said, is practically (i.e., for our
conduct) the same thing as to believe in the non-existence
of God.

Hence, in religious questions we are face to face with
momentous and forced choice; the evasion of choice is itself
a choice in practice for one hypothesis over the other, and is
as momentous as a choice between the hypotheses would be.

Now when we have before us a choice under these conditions, James said that "our passional nature not only law-
fully may, but must, decide." We try to keep wishful thinking out when evidence is available to be weighed. But when
there is not and cannot be evidence and yet we still have to
decide, then we must decide on some grounds other than
evidence. We must decide on the grounds of our motives
which will be affected by our choice, for there are no other
grounds at all.

Religion is a live hypothesis; the choice for it or against
it is momentous; the factual claims for and against it are
inadequately supported by evidence; we cannot avoid affirm-
ing or denying it, since to withhold judgment is in practice
the same as denying it.

Which choice, then, should we make? Many philosophers
would say that their passional nature, what it is that they
"want out of life," would make them choose the path of
agnosticism and atheism; and to those who make this choice,
James conceded that he could not show that they were

mistaken. But his choice was to believe in at least some of the tenets of religion. The consequences of religious belief seemed to him, with his "passional nature" to be definitely better than the consequences of materialism, the belief that he lived in a dead, meaningless, or inimical world in which his moral concerns were illusory and his aspirations necessarily futile;[2] they were better also, he believed, than the consequences of accepting the absolute idealistic conception of the world in which all things are eternally and necessarily good and man's actions are only aspects of some divine logical plan. Such a philosophy—and what James called Spinoza's "block universe" might be taken as typical of either—was to him a debilitating philosophy, without weight of evidence in its favor sufficient to establish it as a truth we must accept willy-nilly.

The opposite—a philosophy in which there is freedom of the will and immortality of the soul, and some friendliness of the universe to man's ideals and highest aspirations, with some looseness or laxness in its structure, so that it does not smother us in its all-embracing goodness—likewise has no objectively valid evidence sufficient to establish it as true. This, James readily admitted. But in its favor, he said, there is this: its acceptance and affirmation have good consequences, moral and emotional. It sets men free from the belief that they are helpless pawns in an inscrutable chess game like the one celebrated by Omar Khayyám, or mere cogs in a world-machine, or actors on a stage senselessly mouthing the lines of a play they do not understand. It makes them feel that they can accomplish something towards the establishment of eternal values; and if they do not feel this, it is certain that they will never achieve it.

Accordingly James made his choice. But he was not dogmatic about it. He warned his readers that he did not profess to show that his choice was necessary to them, though he believed that it was more honest than that of agnostics and atheists, since it opened his mind to evidence and experiences that would be excluded *a priori* by their choice. On the other hand, he warned that he was not declaring an intellectual holiday in which anybody had a right to believe anything he wanted to on any subject: "I do not think," he said, "that any one can accuse me of preaching reckless faith. I have preached [only] the right of the individual to indulge his personal faith at his personal risk."[3]

Let me return for a moment to the two tests for an idea. Has James given us any reason for saying that the consequences of believing in a friendly universe are dependent upon the truth of the proposition that the universe is in fact friendly to our ideals? I do not think that he has done so, but I cannot be sure whether James thought he had done so or not. He called *The Will to Believe* a "sermon on the justification of faith," as if it concerned only the second of the two religious hypotheses, viz., that we are better off here and now for believing that the more perfect is the more eternal. James's argument was, it seems to me, only a recommendation of faith in the absence of knowledge, not a new argument for the truth of the beliefs themselves.

Restricted in this way to the second of the hypotheses, the argument is important. For James correctly saw that unless one did have sufficient belief in an idea to be willing to act upon it, its truth could not be discovered even if it were in fact true. In traditional theological language, James followed St. Anselm in saying that we believe in order that we may know. If we do not believe, we will not get the data or have the experience that could make us know. If we have the minimum amount of belief necessary to permit us to have these experiences and to act upon them, we put ourselves in a position in which one important thing may happen and another important thing will surely happen. Let us consider first what *may* happen, if James's metaphysical conception of reality is correct; for this suggests that James

believed that the pragmatic test of the religious hypothesis
might have the effect of making the religious hypothesis
true.

James's metaphysical doctrine was not one in which the
world exists as an antecedent fixed reality to which we adapt.
It was not for him a ready-made universe, but a universe in
the making, an unfinished universe to which our own activity
is a contribution. Belief leading to action not only affects
the man who believes; it may effect the things believed in,
too. Hope may create its object when its object is something
that can be made real by action. We know this, for instance,
in human society where, James reminds us, the hope for a
woman's love, acted upon, may in fact make the woman love
us. ". . . Faith in a fact can help create the fact . . . ," "The
desire for a certain kind of truth here brings about that
special truth's existence."[4] In a universe that is perpetually
coming to be, is always active through many centers, and has
spirit as the core and not as a useless by-product or illusion,
the world itself may be changed and re-created by human
action in it. "By obstinately believing that there are gods
. . . we are doing the universe the deepest service we can.
. . ."[5] We as it were induce in the world godlike properties
and potentialities. This, however, is wild speculation, neither
theologically nor philosophically very satisfying; and James
was so far from fully elaborating and defending it that one
does not really know to what extent he was brought to it
merely by his enthusiasm for the religious hypothesis.

But if we believe enough in the religious hypothesis to
be susceptible to experiences which bear upon this belief,
another thing will surely happen in and to us if not in and
to the thing we believe in: we can at least get evidence—
James thinks almost scientific evidence—for the religious
hypothesis, *if* there is any such evidence.

The putative evidence was surveyed in James's well-known
lectures, *The Varieties of Religious Experience.* These lec-

tures are mostly on the psychology of religion, and most of them had little or no connection with the religious pragmatism of *The Will to Believe* except for the insistence that willingness to believe is a pre-condition for getting the evidence that may show the religious hypothesis to be at least probable. His procedure in these lectures was not to preach or recommend religious faith on the basis of its good consequences, but rather to examine evidence for or against the existence of the object of faith, as the evidence is found in the religious experiences of individuals.

Religious experiences, especially those of a very vivid kind, often seem to be associated with psychopathology. Many highly and deeply religious persons have been, in the eyes of psychiatrists, victims of hysteria, hallucinations, delusions, and epilepsy. Bertrand Russell once remarked that he could see no more reason for believing that people who have fasted can see real angels flying in the air than for believing that people who have drunk too much whisky can see real rats walking on the ceiling.

James conceded all the facts of psychopathology and added, as well, a large number of weird and fascinating details to the list of symptoms; we are reminded that James was a psychologist and physician before he became a philosopher. Yet he said, rightly, that facts about a person's life are not sufficient to show that his work is valueless or to refute his beliefs. Who would have said that a deaf man like Beethoven could have written beautiful music? Not the otologist, but only the man who had heard the music itself. We listen to Beethoven's music and find it beautiful, and do not say, "It is just sounds put together by a disagreeable old deaf man." Similarly, James said, let us see if what the abnormal, perhaps unbalanced, religious people say makes any sense. He asked: Is the religious experience, as reported by mystics and seers, consistent enough to support a hypothesis about what it is that they claim to have experienced? And he answered that it was.

In all the manifold and confusing variety of religious experiences preserved in both Christian and non-Christian religious literature, James found certain common traits. The most important of these were:

First, the religious person initially has a feeling of uneasiness and emptiness in the ordinary experiences of his life, a sense of sin, impotence, abandonedness, meaninglessness. In the most religious, there is what James called "the sick soul."

Second, this feeling is replaced by another feeling that the sufferer is "making proper connection with the higher powers."

Third, there occurs an identification of himself with the higher part of himself that exists in this connection with the higher powers.

And fourth, "He becomes conscious that this higher part is conterminous and continuous with a MORE of the same quality, which is operative in the universe outside of him, and which he can keep in working touch with, and in a fashion get on board of and save himself when all his lower being has gone to pieces in the wreck."[6]

Each of these traits of religious experience was documented by James from hundreds of reports of mystical experiences, conversions, rebirths, prayer, and worship. He chose to accept in their light what he called the "overbelief" that what is experienced in these ways—this higher self conterminous and continuous with something external— really exists. That is, he concluded that the religious experience, regardless of its often pathological origin, had evidential value.

What it was evidence for, however, was not so clear. Each mystic in describing his own ineffable experience cannot help using the vocabulary of his particular religious culture and education, so that when he came to deal with specific points of their revelations, James found that the descriptions of the religious experiences diverged after they had traveled along in unison through the four points listed above. And, of course, each one diverged in the direction of the theological system familiar to the particular mystic.

James's own hypothesis, however, did not conform to that of traditional Christianity. He tried to frame a hypothesis that would account for the common traits of religious experience without going to the extremes of any particular one. And he concluded that the simplest hypothesis adequate to the "practical needs and experiences" of religion was not monotheism or pantheism but polytheism. He wrote:

. . . Beyond each man and in a fashion continuous with him there exists a larger power that is friendly to him and to his ideals. All that the facts [of religious experience] require is that the power should be both other and larger than our conscious selves. Anything larger will do, if only it be large enough to trust for the next step [beyond our own individuality]. It need not be infinite, it need not be solitary. It might conceivably be only a larger and more godlike self, of which the present self would be but the mutilated expression, and the universe might conceivably be a collection of such selves, of different degrees of inclusiveness, with no absolute unity realized in it at all. Thus would a sort of polytheism return upon us. . . .[7]

Polytheism has always had an appeal to philosophers who, like James, take the problem of evil seriously and who are strongly activistic and individualistic in their outlook. James had always rejected monism, a philosophy that all things are ultimately one; he called monism the belief in a "block universe." James did not object only to the block universe of the materialists, to whom we are all cogs in a machine, or to that of Spinoza, which is a tightly knit logical whole; he objected likewise to the block universe of the absolute idealists for whom everything exists in a spiritual absolute of

supreme values. When he was writing, it was commonly
believed that this conception of the universe, derived ultimately from Hegel, was the one most appropriate to religion.
But James saw that a universe in which evil is considered
partial good and necessary to the whole is a universe in
which the connectedness of all things, including oneself,
leaves no elbowroom for adventure, creativity, and initiative,
without which there is no good in a human sense at all.
The universe of the absolute idealists was thought by him to
be inhospitable to our experiences of good and evil as funda-
mentally different, and inhospitable to our responsibility for
working to bring about the gradual triumph of the former
over the latter.

James therefore put against this conception a pluralistic
theory in which God is a being within the universe, with
other beings outside Him, in part independent of Him and
in part, perhaps, even inimical to Him. God is not an Absolute Self; even the words he thought to be nonsensical,
since a self has always a nonself over against it, as environment, challenge, and opportunity. Only as a being in the
world, and not as equivalent to the All, can God be considered as a person and as an appropriate object for religious
experience, sentiment, and activity.

This is a conception which is not only polytheistic but
involves the notion of a finite god or gods with whom man
can enter into active relations. It has had a long history in
philosophy, beginning at least as far back as Plato. The
most eloquent expression of it is found in a statement by
John Stuart Mill, which James could have repeated—were
he given to repeating other philosophers—without wishing to
change a word:

One elevated feeling this form of religious idea admits of,
which is not open to those who believe in the omnipotence of
the good principle in the universe, [namely] the feeling of help-
ing God—of requiting the good he has given by a voluntary co-

operation which he, not being omnipotent, really needs, and by which a somewhat nearer approach may be made to the fulfilment of his purposes. . . . To do something during life, on even the humblest scale if nothing more is within reach, towards bringing this consummation ever so little nearer, is the most animating and invigorating thought which can inspire a human creature, . . .[8]

SUGGESTED READINGS

Many of James's works are available in inexpensive editions, including the *Varieties. The Philosophy of William James*, edited by Horace M. Kallen (New York: Modern Library, 1925) is a useful collection. The best study of James's life and philosophy is the Pulitzer Prize-winning *Thought and Character of William James* (2 vols.) by Ralph Barton Perry (Boston: Little, Brown, 1935); cf. also Perry's shorter book, *In the Spirit of William James* (New Haven: Yale University Press, 1938). J. S. Bixler's *Religion in the Philosophy of William James* (Boston: Marshall Jones Co., 1926) and Santayana's chapter on James in *Character and Opinion in the United States* (New York: Charles Scribner's Sons, 1920) may be recommended.

VIII

Santayana

There is no God, and the Virgin Mary is His Mother." . . . Santayana did not say this; it was jokingly attributed to him by Bertrand Russell. But he might have said it; it is like some of his epigrams, and it almost epitomizes his philosophy of religion. It brings into vivid juxtaposition the two poles of his thought on religion: a skepticism or negativism towards so-called religious truth, and an affirmation of the values inherent in religious faith and practice.

George Santayana was born in Spain in 1863 and was brought to America at the age of nine. He was educated at Harvard and in Germany, and he became a colleague of James at Harvard during the greatest days of Harvard philosophy. He was never entirely comfortable in America; he, somewhat like Henry James, was alien to almost all the aspects of American life of which William James was the philosophical spokesman. Like Henry James, therefore, he spent most of his life in Europe. He died in Rome in 1952.

Santayana's style of writing may have stood in the way of his gaining the fame he deserved as a philosophical writer, but it brought him fame as a man of letters. Not only was he poet and novelist and essayist; he was a philosopher whose strictly philosophical works were written in a style that made them accessible to the layman, and some people no doubt had the illusion, forgetting Plato and Hume, that a philosopher easy to read must be superficial in thought. That his

106

three-volume autobiography showed him mostly in the role of an aristocratic man of the world amusedly contemptuous of professors did not help his reputation as a serious thinker. Yet in technical philosophical debate with his peers —James, Russell, John Dewey—he was a master of the difficult philosophic craft, a master who is not and should not be forgotten in the history of Anglo-Saxon philosophy.

His most important writings, for our purposes, were *Reason in Religion*, which was the third volume of his *Life of Reason*, and *The Idea of Christ in the Gospels*. The first was published in 1906, the second forty years later. It is remarkable how little essential difference there is between the two books. We can move back and forth between them without much danger of anachronism, but there is in the second of them a greater richness of historical and theological detail, and a more intimate appreciation of Christianity and its differences from other religions.

Santayana's general philosophical position may best be called naturalism. In an earlier day it would have been called materialism; perhaps it still should be. But in the twentieth century, materialism has come to be the name of a kind of naturalism that Santayana rejected because it was, in his opinion and that of other naturalists, like Dewey, much too simple. Materialists throughout history have been followers of Democritus, who saw the world as a blind and meaningless concourse of atoms in the void, with all the color and savor and value of life as somehow illusory or less real than the measurable physico-chemical properties of things. Materialists have almost always been mechanists; they believed in a world-machine governed by the laws of the pushes and pulls of its minute particles. We understand more complicated phenomena only by reducing them to their lowest, physical terms. Life, for them, is merely the name we give to a physico-chemical phenomenon of almost incredible complexity. Consciousness is only a kind of internal shadow of what goes on in the brain, and like all shadows it is ineffective in the course of events. Words like "good" and "beautiful" only name those shadows that have a tint of pleasure; they have no reference to the effective powers and laws of reality.

Modern naturalists are often called materialists by their critics. But they reply that such a mechanistic materialism as I have just described is far too speculative in one direction, and far too simple in another. Too speculative, because it accepts the results of science as having metaphysical authority and finality, and does not remember the essentially temporary and tentative character of scientific hypotheses; too simple, because the materialist chooses only a small part of the data of experience, those of the physical sciences, and ignores or explains away the rest of it.

The naturalists accept whatever they find, even moral ideals and aspirations, as products of nature and as revealing symptoms of her fecundity. The natural order is not, for them, the world of physics, with the facts of biology, psychology, anthropology, history, art, and religion merely illusory glosses upon it. All these facts are parts of nature, which is the realm of what *is* whether it fits the formulae of physics or not; *every* picture of the world, including the scientific, is an abstraction from the rich store of reality. Reality is still called "matter" by Santayana, but his matter is not just the stuff that physics used to deal with.

To be a naturalist means to try to find the origin and occasion and value of all things in an order of nature which we can learn to know only by investigating all its fruits, in all the fields of culture. To be a naturalist means to refuse to set in opposition to each other two realms of discourse, one marked "nature" and the other marked "culture." "Nature produces culture just as soil produces flowers," said one of Santayana's followers. Everything is to be understood by recourse to the executive order of nature. But the categories for this understanding must be discovered in an open-minded investigation of all that comes before us in experience, and not by an *a priori* decision in favor of those of the natural sciences.

What reality itself is, if defined more specifically than "whatever appears in its manifold variety," remains hidden from us. Even our scientific portrait of nature is a product of a social and poetizing process; the physical world-picture is as much a self-portrait of the scientific mind as it is a portrait of nature considered as something given in brute fact. The scientist's faith in a stable and simple external order of laws is as much a product of reason's need and imagination as a religious or mythological system is. Nature understood by the scientists has no prerogative over nature understood through other media equally natural for the cultivation of reason; and "matter" is too good a word for the physical scientist to be permitted to monopolize it. Each picture of nature has its use, responsive to the need which made us produce it. Skepticism of the objective truth of any of our pictures of nature, and animal faith in what is their objective origin, are the two poles of Santayana's epistemology.

Such a philosopher could be expected to have the ambivalence towards religion shown in the epigram with which I began. Santayana's study of religion is a way of getting at an understanding of man and nature, not a path to any truths about a world which is not natural at all, but supernatural. Earlier materialists—whom Santayana referred to as "young wits and worm-eaten satirists"—had recognized the all-too-human elements in religion and had emphasized them in deprecating the claims of religion to be true. Voltaire had spoken of the necessity of inventing a God if one did not exist; Marx had called religion the opium of the people; Hume had shown the predominant role of fear in the creation of the idea of God; Haeckel had just recently poured his scorn on religious anthropomorphism by referring to God as a "gaseous vertebrate." But all these thinkers (with the possible exception of Hume) had started out not only with an antireligious bias but, more importantly, with an eighteenth-century caricature of man as a rational animal for whom literal truth was the only alternative to folly and superstition. By this oversimplification, Santayana said, they left unexplored "the habits of thought from which those tenets [of religion] sprang, their original meaning, and their true function."[1] Precisely this humane investigation of the nature, origin, function, and validity of religious thought was undertaken by Santayana. Something very much like it had just been performed by Nietzsche, but with a rancor and prophetic spleen wholly uncongenial to the aloof sympathy with which Santayana looked upon human affairs, including human ignorance and folly.

Santayana traced the life of reason in five spheres: common sense, society, religion, art, and science. Reason for Santayana was a completely natural aspect of experience, which was itself an outgrowth of a natural evolution. It is experience become reflective and efficacious in the preservation and production of its own values. It is thought bringing about a felt synthesis of impulse and ideal by producing images which are responses to natural needs. It disciplines impulse and focuses it in images of ideal values which can be partially realized and enjoyed in further experience. An object, such as this table before me, is known only as an image which reason has synthesized out of all sorts of sensory contents, following the natural need of having before me stable objects with which I can work and on which I can depend in planning my further actions. Even the table, therefore, is an image representing some part of the ideal of a stable world in which practical experience can be managed pragmatically. The life of reason is practical thought and action, which is justified by its fruits in experience. This fruit is the enjoyment of excellence in both impulse and image, whether the impulse be to have something stable before me on which to place a book or to have some ideal goal at which to direct my life, and whether the image be a table, a work of art, a state, a molecule, or the Kingdom of God.

All of these are images or myths, produced by need but expressing an idealization of imagination and reason. In the life of reason fully realized, ideals cease to be merely visionary and become operative; impulses cease to be merely brutish and become human; actions cease to be spasmodic and vain, and become intelligent and effective. The life of reason itself is the concrete natural ideal of a conscious being like man. It is not just a means to some other end, as it appeared to some pragmatists to be; it is itself the origin and locus of the celebration of all value. Living the life of reason is the highest and only genuine good of a being like man, who is actually animal but potentially rational.

Religion is one sphere of the life of reason. It grows out of our social life with its moral demands. "It makes absolute moral decisions"—not just those of prudence. "It sanctions, unifies, and transforms ethics"—freeing it from the merely local and temporal, and giving it what appears to be an eternal and absolute dimension. It emancipates us, in part, from our personal limitations. All phases of the life of reason do this to some extent, for we cannot be reasonable and remain wholly immersed in our little private glob of experience. We become reasonable by leaving, at least in imagination and in planning our actions, the place we are in, not by remaining stuck in it with the illusion that it and we are the center of the universe. Religion does these things through its mythology and poetry: "Religion pursues rationality through the imagination."

"The only truth of religion," continued our philosopher, "comes from its interpretation of life, from its symbolic rendering of that aspiration which it springs out of and which it seeks to illuminate." But through an insidious but natural misunderstanding—Santayana will have nothing of the chicanery of priests to explain what he thinks is a natural illusion of all mankind—which it can outgrow only through philosophy, the poetry of religion is not recognized as poetry. Rather, it is thought of as literal truth and as having an independent and supernatural moral authority. The falsehood of religion, therefore, is the belief that "these poetic conceptions are not merely poetical, but are literal information about experience and reality elsewhere—an experience and reality which, strangely enough, supply just those defects displayed by reality and experience here."[2]

To believe that the religious poetry and myth is literally true is not just a harmless fancy; such a belief limits and threatens our moral and intellectual freedom. Morally, it distorts the relation between man and nature, and makes him despise nature, including his own, by locating that which is most worthful in a non-natural (and therefore unreal) ideal realm where it is ineffective; in Nietzsche's language, the literal view of religion destroys the innocence of existence, out of which, Santayana thought, religion itself has grown. And intellectually it is hazardous, because the myths are not true, and when this is discovered, as it always is, there is a disillusionment which will not recognize that there is something wiser in religion than factual truth could ever be. It jeopardizes the excellences which religion has embodied in its poetry, because it occasions a harping on its literal falseness, which would never have been necessary if men had not ignorantly believed at first that there was literal truth in it. Not to throw the baby out with the bath, therefore, we must "rediscover the origin of the gods, reduce them analytically to their natural and moral constituents, and then proceed to rearrange these materials, without any quantitative loss, in forms appropriate to a maturer reflection."[3] The essential words here are: "without any quantitative loss"—but Santayana might have written, "without any qualitative loss," for his is not a program of debunking religion.

Our ancestors made poetry and myth to express their interpretation of life, their wisdom, just as we do. They used mythical forms because they had no others; we use mythical forms, in novels and dramas, because we have no others so appropriate. But whereas we do not generally mistake our own poetic myths for facts—nobody even cares, unless he be a pedant, whether Hamlet ever lived or not—the mistake has ever since been made of seeing the essence of religion in the letter of the ancestral myths and not in the wisdom which was their root. The error has been repeatedly made of insisting upon belief in the myth while forgetting the wisdom it taught. Every viable myth in religion has a profound human insight as its source. Men's images of the gods are so many interpretations of the human heart and its predicaments. The very existence of these images is a symptom of our ineradicable feelings of dependence on something not ourselves and of our need of affinity with what we depend upon. These feelings are given appropriate human expression only in the images of kinship, dominion, justice, mercy, glory, wisdom, love, and the like.

In each ingredient in the religious myth, Santayana tried to find a moral reflection upon the human situation; "Religions," he said, "are the great fairy tales of conscience." For the impotence of the creature, there is the chastening awareness that we are in the hands of inscrutable power; hence man proposes, but God disposes. For the awareness that earthly fortunes are indeed precarious, there is first the myth of the jealousy of the gods and then the notion of the transitoriness of all things temporal here, where rust doth corrupt. For the desperate awareness of need for help in work that lies beyond human power, there is prayer. For mundane injustice, there is the myth of the mills of the gods.

Originally, perhaps, religion and morality were separate and even antithetical, as Hume believed; but by first believing in the magical efficacy of good works, men subsequently gave a moral efficacy to religion.[4] The religious image and symbolism in each case can be held vividly before us, and we are constantly reminded, in the forgetful press of life, of the wisdom that we do not exist by our own power, that our work flourishes only in circumstances we cannot survey, that pride cometh before a fall, that no man is an island unto himself. It is these lessons that we know, but forget, which are made memorable and at least partially effective in the life of reason by being clothed in the unforgettable imagery of religion.

Each of the great religions of mankind has its own mythology, expressing the moral discoveries of its founders and the needs of its adherents who are loyal to its poetry. Because some needs and bafflements are universally human, the religions all teach much the same wisdom, but in different myths. Religions do not differ as true or false, but as better or worse for the enshrinement of reason in the pursuit and enjoyment of value. Nothing is gained, however, by the attempt to exchange one's own religion for a better one, for the moral truths of an accepted religious fable have a hold that rationalistic critique cannot entirely loose. While it is an accident that one is born a Christian rather than a Buddhist, or a Catholic rather than a Protestant, Santayana has only impatient contempt for those who shop around among sects, or try to pick and choose what they will believe and what they will reject in a sect to which they belong and to which they have a far deeper than merely intellectual commitment. The religions that now live have survived because they met the moral needs of their people in their circumstances; tampering with religious forms weakens and does not improve the functions of religion.

Thus he compared the Anglican Church to the English public school: it is an instrument "of a beautiful integration: . . . something voluminous, comfortable, and sane, on a political, conventional, and sporting level"[5]—in a word, something very very British. His own allegience, however, was to the Catholic Church, and to the Catholic Church which fought the modernist heresy,[6] not to the Catholics who tried to compromise with modernism: ". . . The Catholic form is as good as any intrinsically for the devotee himself, and it has immense advantages over its probable rivals in charm, in comprehensiveness, in maturity, in internal rationality, in external adaptability, . . ."[7] Yet how superciliously tolerant Santayana could be! "I almost share," he said, "that 'extraordinary faith in the moral efficacy of cold baths and dumb-bells' which Mr. Bertrand Russell attributes to the Y.M.C.A. Sport, companionship, reading-rooms, with an occasional whiff of religious sentiment to stop foul mouths and turn aside hard questions—all this composes a saving tonic for the simple masculine soul habitually in the service of Big Business, . . ."[8]

Santayana's detached tolerance, of course, extended also to non-Christian religions, and some of his critics have found him more of a quietistic Buddhist than an activistic Christian; certain it is that he was little concerned with social reforms and philanthropy characteristically Christian, and was contemptuous of the modernists who were more concerned with the fact that men were unhappy than with the fact that they were sinful. Yet in an earlier work, *Interpretations of Poetry and Religion,* he had tried to explain the spread of Christianity at the expense of its early rivals, and had done so in terms of its greater adequacy to deal with the human predicament.

Only Christianity, he said of the early days of the Church, could succeed because it alone had all that was needed: roots in the faith of a singularly religious people, the Jews; a supernaturalism that left scope for poetic creation; a Scripture hallowed by tradition, so that it could preserve its identity through the critical centuries; a direct contact with the individual without a political apparatus; and, most of all, an impetus to moral self-criticism and individual moral reform that were lacking in the more easygoing pagan religions. Christianity had all the advantages—a new poetry, a new moral ideal, and an old God. Christianity alone among its rivals could transmute all the facts of life into moral lessons and relate them all to a single center: the death of Christ on the cross, not the death of Socrates from hemlock, could become a religious inspiration, because "Christ's death is a symbol of human life. Men could 'believe in' his death because it was a figure and premonition of their experience."[9]

It was the moral significance of the mythical interpretation of the crucifixion as suffering and renunciation, which is the subject matter of poetry, rather than the factual significance of the literal statement of one man's death, which is the subject matter of history, that gives substance to Christianity and provides it with the occasion for poetry that seems to be more than poetry. A religion with such poetry as this is in its essence unaffected by mere historical or scientific criticism of the facts. No religion can last if it is merely temporal, local, historical, and factual in its teaching; it must teach the essential, and make it seem eternal. "Human life," wrote Santayana, "is always essentially the same, and therefore a religion which, like Christianity, seizes the essence of that life, ought to be an eternal religion."[10]

Santayana narrated this essential Christian myth in his book *The Idea of Christ in the Gospels*. It is the idea of God in man. The ultimate myth, of course, is God himself. "I set up no gods," said Santayana in his address on the tercentenary of Spinoza's birth. But ". . . I do consider on what subjects and to what end we might consult those gods, if we found that they existed: and surely the aspiration that would prompt us, in that case, to worship the gods, would be our truest heart-bond and our ultimate religion."[11]

"God" is Santayana's name for the collective good of the universe, focused as a single image. The central tenet of Christianity is that this ultimate and perfect good appeared once in human form without destroying the humanity, but fulfilling it; it is the mythical image for the aspiration of man to be godlike, the image itself being God-become-man.

The idea of Christianity is that God was in man, and the moral root and consequence of this idea is that goodness "may be exemplified in some degree in anybody, as we find it so perfectly exemplified in Christ."[12] The meaning of Christ on the cross is not that Christ died for our sins as a scapegoat or sacrifice; that is only the poetic image taken literally as representing superstitious magic. The crucifixion did not work salvation automatically, as the New Testament repeatedly shows. Only to those who believed, the crucifixion brought salvation of the spirit by working "a change of allegiance in [their] heart, so that the interests of the world will count for less and less in the heart, and the interests of the spirit for more and more."[13]

Once again Santayana emphasized the difference between the wisdom embodied here and literal truth. It might sometimes be hard to decide, in reading his last book on religion, whether he had indeed become a "believer" in the sense of believing that the Christian interpretation of the life of Jesus was literally true. Many pages of the book are written as if they were meant to be elaborations of historical or theological truths; it is not the sort of book that we can easily imagine a real skeptic having the patience or talent to write. Yet the question that we might want to ask Santayana has no explicit answer in the book; he only refers us to his views as expressed elsewhere. If we ask, is the teaching of the Christian religion true, or is it only better (if it is) than that of, say, the Greek mythology, Santayana would say the question is not important enough to merit an answer:

As in poetry, so in religion, the question whether the events described have actually occurred is trivial and irrelevant. . . . Facts matter little for the spirit except what they mean for the heart. . . . Lucifer might admit that a divine Christ had existed, yet might disdain to imitate him; and a disillusioned philosopher might aspire to imitate him without believing in his existence.[14]

But when we turn from the problem of the historicity or even the divinity of Christ to Santayana's final metaphysics, there is no doubt where he stands with respect to the "ghostly physics" of theology. There is an *ens realissimum*, a most real being in the light of which everything else is to be explained. Spinoza called this *ens realissimum* substance, *deus sive natura*. Even atheists, said Santayana, believe there is an *ens realissimum*, and the only question between atheists and theists is a semantic one: does the ultimate metaphysical reality deserve the name 'God'? Spinoza believed it did; Santayana believed it did not. The *ens realissimum* for him was matter, which is the origin of spirit and not its product. "In respect to popular religion that thinks of God as the creator of the world and the dispenser of fortune," he said at the end of his *magnum opus* in metaphysics, "my philosophy is atheistic."[15] To avoid the charge of atheism by worship of the *ens realissimum*, i.e., to call matter 'God' and worship it, "inverts the natural order" in which spirit with its awareness of the good arises out of nature and poetically and morally projects an ideal and calls *it* God.

The ontological argument was right in its premise: God is a perfect being. But its conclusion is wrong, for God does not exist in any sense other than as a creation of spirit.

Suggested Readings

Santayana is his own best expositor, and several of his works, e.g., *Interpretations of Poetry and Religion*, are available in inexpensive paperback editions. *The Life of Reason* and *Realms of Being* are now available in one-volume editions (Scribner's). A good selection of his work is given by Irwin Edman in *The Philosophy of Santayana* (New York: Random House—Modern Library, n.d.). Santayana's autobiography, *Persons and Places*, 3 vols. (New York: Charles Scribner's Sons, 1944-53), is fascinating. Also recommended: George W. Howgate, *George Santayana* (Philadelphia: University of Pennsylvania Press, 1938) and Milton K. Munitz, *The Moral Philosophy of Santayana* (New York: Columbia University Press, 1939).

Notes

Chapter I. *What Is Secular Philosophy?*

1. Pope Pius XII, in the encyclical *Humani Generis* (1950) wrote: "You may deck out philosophy in more elaborate garments, and such as are more becoming to it; you may fortify it with more telling terminology; you may relieve it of an ill-conceived argument, here and there, which the schoolmen have brought forward in its defense; you may enrich it, if due caution be observed, with certain new elements which the progress of human thought has brought with it. But whatever you do, you must not uproot it, you must not adulterate it with false principles, you must not treat it as an interesting ruin. Truth, and the philosophic expression of truth, cannot change in a night. We are dealing with those principles of thought which impose themselves, in their own right, on the human mind; We are speaking of conclusions which are based on the wisdom of the ages, and for that matter on the coincident support of divine revelation. The mind of man, when it is engaged in a sincere search for truths, will never light on one which contradicts the truths it has already ascertained. God is truth itself; He it is who has created, and who directs, the human intellect." (Quoted from *The Papal Encyclicals*, edited by Anne Freemantle [New York: New American Library, Mentor Book, 1956], p. 286.)

2. "Secularism" is often lumped together with "materialism" and "scientism" by defenders of religion. For instance, in a statement by the Administrative Board of the National Catholic Welfare Conference (*New York Times*, Nov. 16, 1958, p. 70) we find the following: "The basic tenets of these ideologies [materialism and secularism] is that man's real concern is with the here and now, with the actual politics and economics of this world, to the exclusion, theoretical or practical, of the things

119

of the spirit and their relegation to the realm of pure fantasy."
This is not the way I use the term "secularism" in this book.
This sentence has little or no application to the philosophers discussed here. The "ideology of secularism," if I may borrow the
word, is in my opinion merely this: All beliefs, including religious beliefs, are worthy of acceptance if, and only if, philosophical scrutiny recommends them; the authority of whoever teaches
them is not sufficient to warrant their acceptability. Materialists are, by this definition, secularists (unless, indeed, they
take their materialism from a blind Marxist faith); but a secu-
larist need not be a materialist, and none of the philosophers discussed in this book was a materialist. "Scientism" would be the
"ideology" that would give the judicative function to the
sciences, not to philosophy.

Chapter II. *Families of Secular Philosophers*

1. George Santayana, *The Life of Reason* (one-volume ed.,
New York: Chas. Scribner's Sons, 1954), p. 184.

Chapter III. *Spinoza*

1. "On the Improvement of the Understanding," *Chief
Works*, trans. R. H. M. Elwes (London: George Bell & Sons,
1887), Vol. II, p. 1. (All quotations from Spinoza are from
this edition.)
2. "Theological-Political Tractate," Vol. I, p. 187.
3. *Ibid.*, pp. 258-9.
4. *Ibid.*, p. 262.
5. *Ethics*, Book I, Appendix (Vol. II, p. 78.)
6. William Pepperell Montague, *Great Visions of Philosophy*
(La Salle: Open Court, 1950), p. 17.
7. *Ethics*, Book V, Proposition XLII, Note (Vol. II, pp.
270-1).

Chapter IV. *Hume*

1. Letter from Adam Smith to William Strahan, November 9,
1776. This letter was published in 1777 together with Hume's
autobiography.

2. *An Inquiry Concerning Human Understanding,* edited by Charles W. Hendel (New York: Liberal Arts Press, 1955), p. 173.

3. *Ibid.,* p. 140.

4. *Ibid.,* p. 123.

5. *Ibid.,* p. 125.

6. *Ibid.,* p. 124.

7. "Dialogues Concerning Natural Religion," *Hume Selections,* ed. Hendel (New York: Chas. Scribner's Sons, 1927), pp. 302-3. All subsequent page references are to this volume.

8. *Ibid.,* p. 310.

9. *Ibid.,* p. 309.

10. *Ibid.,* p. 332.

11. *Ibid.,* p. 332.

12. *Ibid.,* p. 401.

13. "The Natural History of Religion," p. 279.

14. *Ibid.,* p. 280-1.

15. *Ibid.,* p. 277.

16. "Dialogues Concerning Natural Religion," pp. 394-5.

17. "The Natural History of Religion," p. 283.

Chapter V. *Kant*

1. Johann Gottfried Herder, "Briefe zu Beförderung der Humanität" (1792). *Sämmtliche Werke,* ed. Suphan, Vol. XVIII, pp. 324-5. [Trans. Beck]

2. C. D. Broad, *Religion, Philosophy, and Psychical Research,* (New York: Harcourt, Brace and Co., 1953), pp. 182-3.

3. *Critique of Pure Reason,* trans. Norman Kemp Smith (New York: Macmillan and Co., 1929), p. 520.

4. *Ibid.,* p. 29.

5. *Critique of Practical Reason,* trans. L. W. Beck (New York: Liberal Arts Press, 1956), p. 152.

6. *Ibid.,* p. 134.

7. *Religion within the Limits of Reason Alone,* trans. H. H. Hudson and T. M. Greene (New York: Harper & Brothers, 1960), pp. 90 ff.

8. *Ibid.,* p. 158.

9. "What is Enlightenment?" in *Foundations of the Metaphysics of Morals*, trans. L. W. Beck (New York: Liberal Arts Press, 1959), p. 88.

Chapter VI. *Nietzsche*

1. "Thus Spoke Zarathustra," *The Portable Nietzsche*, p. 139.
2. *Ibid.*, p. 230.
3. "Toward a Geneaology of Morals," I, §10, *The Portable Nietzsche*, p. 451; *The Philosophy of Nietzsche* (Modern Library ed.), p. 17.
4. *The Will to Power*, §179, trans. A. M. Ludovici in *The Complete Works of Friedrich Nietzsche*, ed. by Oscar Levy (New York: Macmillan and Co., 1924), Vol. XIV.
5. "Beyond Good and Evil," §62, *The Philosophy of Nietzsche*, p. 70.
6. "Genealogy," III, §27, *Ibid.*, p. 175.
7. "Zarathustra," *The Portable Nietzsche*, pp. 123-4.
8. "The Antichrist," §39, *Ibid.*, p. 612.
9. *The Will to Power*, §§168, 158.
10. "Genealogy," III, §22, *The Philosophy of Nietzsche*, p. 157.
11. "Zarathustra," *The Portable Nietzsche*, p. 185.
12. "The Antichrist," §62, *Ibid.*, pp. 655-6.
13. Quoted from Kaufmann, *Nietzsche*, p. 271. The following paragraph is largely based on Kaufmann's reconciliation of the doctrines of the Superman and eternal recurrence, which many writers have believed to be inconsistent with each other.
14. "Zarathustra (The Drunken Song)" §12, *The Portable Nietzsche*, p. 436. Copyright 1954 by The Viking Press, Inc., and quoted by permission of Walter Kaufmann and The Viking Press, Inc. Kaufmann has given another translation of this song in his *Nietzsche*.

Chapter VIII. *James*

1. *Pragmatism* (New York: Longmans, Green, and Co., 1909), p. 222.
2. But Bertrand Russell, with *his* "passional nature," drew just

the opposite conclusion from the belief that we do indeed live in a dead, meaningless, or inimical world. Instead of being dispirited by it, or seeking the right to believe (as James did) in some power in the universe friendly to our highest aspirations, he called on man "to sustain alone, a weary but unyielding Atlas, the world that his own ideals have fashioned despite the trampling march of unconscious power" ("A Free Man's Worship" [1903], reprinted in *Mysticism and Logic* [New York: Doubleday & Co.—Anchor Book, 1957]).

3. *The Will to Believe* (New York: Longmans, Green, and Co., 1917), p. xi.

4. *Ibid.*, pp. 25, 24; cf. *A Pluralistic Universe* (New York: Longmans, Green, and Co., 1909), p. 329.

5. *The Will to Believe*, p. 28.

6. *The Varieties of Religious Experience* (New York: The Modern Library, n.d.), pp. 498-9.

7. *Ibid.*, p. 515.

8. John Stuart Mill, *Three Essays on Religion* (New York: Henry Holt, 1874), p. 256.

CHAPTER VIII. *Santayana*

1. *The Life of Reason*, p. 179.

2. *Ibid.*, p. 183.

3. *Ibid.*, p. 206.

4. *Ibid.*, pp. 195, 198, 213 ff.

5. *The Genteel Tradition at Bay* (New York: Chas. Scribner's Sons, 1931), p. 71.

6. *Winds of Doctrine* (New York: Chas. Scribner's Sons, 1913), Chap. 2.

7. *Ibid.*, p. 56.

8. *The Genteel Tradition at Bay*, pp. 70-71.

9. *Interpretations of Poetry and Religion* (New York: Chas. Scribner's Sons, 1900), p. 93.

10. *Ibid.*, p. 116.

11. "Ultimate Religion," *The Philosophy of Santayana* (Modern Library ed.), p. 592.

12. *The Idea of Christ in the Gospels* (New York: Chas. Scribner's Sons, 1946), p. 86.

13. *Ibid.*, p. 152.
14. *Ibid.*, pp. 173-174.
15. *Realms of Being* (New York: Chas. Scribner's Sons, 1942), p. 838.

INDEX

Agnosticism, 25, 42
Aiken, Henry D., 60
"Animal faith," 109
Anselm, St., 64, 99
Anthropomorphism, 53, 56 ff., 76, 109
Aquinas, St. Thomas, 12 f., 67, 72
Argument from design, 48 ff., 51 ff., 64, 67
Aristotle, 17
Atheism, 9, 23, 27, 42, 85 f., 118
Autonomy, moral and political, 70, 73

Beethoven, 101
Belief, analysis of, 10; *see also* Faith
Bergson, Henri, 81
Bible, 33, 75, 86 f.; Higher criticism of, 31 ff.
Bixler, J. S., 105
"Block universe," 98
Boswell, James, 42
Broad, C. D., 65
Browne, Lewis, 41
Burtt, E. A., 26, 41

Causation, Hume on, 43
Charles V., 81
Christianity, 73, 86, 115, and *passim*
Church invisible, 74 ff.
Church and state, 34, 88
Cicero, 53 n.
Common, Thomas, 90
Comte, Auguste, 14
Cosmological Argument, 53, 64, 66 ff.

Darwin, Charles, 22, 79
Deism, 56 ff.
Democritus, 107
Descartes, Rene, 64
Dewey, John, 107
de Witt, Jan, 31
Divine law, 33 ff., 38
Dostoevski, 87

Edman, Irwin, 118

Empiricism, 43
England, F. E., 78
Epicurus, 53 n.
Eternal recurrence, 89, 122
Ethical commonwealth, 74 f.
Evil, Problem of, 53 f., 103

Faith, 12 ff., 68, 71 ff., 84, 99 ff.
Faust, 90
Freedom of thought, 34 f., 77 f.
Freemantle, Anne, 119
Freud, Sigmund, 81
Friedrich Wilhelm II, 63

Gibbon, Edward, 42, 59
God, 37 ff., 116, 118, and *passim;* Intellectual love of, 39 ff.
Greene, T. M., 77
Gutmann, James, 41

Haeckel, Ernst, 109
Hegel, G. W. F., 104
Heine, Heinrich, 27, 63
Hendel, C. W., 59
Herder, J. G., 62
Hobbes, Thomas, 92
Howgate, G. W., 118
Humanism, 23
Hume, David, 19, 20 f., 23, 25, 27, chap. iv, 61, 63, 68, 92, 93, 106, 109, 113
Huxley, T. H., 42

Idealism, Absolute, 103
Immoralism, 80 f.
"Innocence of existence," 79, 88, 112

James, Henry, 92, 106
James, William, 19, 23, 24 f., chap. vii, 106, 107
Jesus, 27, 87, 117
Job, 54
Johnson, Samuel, 42
Judaism, 83 ff., 86

125

Kallen, H. M., 105
Kant, Immanuel, 19, 21 ff., 23 f., 25, 35, 51, 52, chap. v, 92
Kaufmann, Walter, 26, 90, 91
Kemp Smith, Norman, 60
Kolbenheyer, E. G., 41
Körner, S., 77 f.
Kroner, Richard, 78

Laplace, 52, 61
Leibniz, G. W. von, 13, 30
Lindsay, A. D., 78
Locke, John, 13, 35, 45

Marx, Karl, 109
Materialism, 23, 98, 107 f., 119
Mechanism, 36, 46
Mennonites, 31
Methodism, 61
Mill, J. S., 35, 104
Milton, John, 35
Miracle, 36, 46 ff.
Modernism, 115
Monism, 36 f.
Monotheism, 54, 57
Montagu, Lady Mary, 42
Montague, W. P., 37
Moral argument, 71
Morgan, G. A., 79, 91
Mossner, E. C., 60
Mozart, 81
Munitz, M. K., 118
Mystical experience, 102
Myth, 112 ff.

Napoleon, 47, 81
Naturalism, 107 ff.
Newton, Sir Isaac, 52
Nietzsche, F., 19, 22 ff., 25, chap. vi, 110, 112
Nihilism, 85
Novalis, 27

Omar Khayyám, 98
Ontological argument, 64 ff., 118
Over-belief, 26

Pantheism, 38
Paul, St., 79, 87, 88
Perry, R. B., 105
Philosophy: defined, 16; its relation to religion, 11 ff.
Pietism, 61
Pius XII, Pope, 119
Plato, 35, 51, 106
Platonism, 44, 56
Pluralism, 93, 104

Polytheism, 54, 103
Positivism, 14 f., 94
Powell, E. E., 41
Pragmatism, 92 ff., 110
Prayer, 76, 113
Providence, 49
Psychoanalysis, 15

Quakers 31

Rationalism, 43, 45, 50
Reformation, 12
Religion: definitions of, 9, 72; primitive, 56 ff.
"Religion of humanity," 14
Religious experience, 101 ff.
Resentment, 82 ff.
Revelation, 12 f., 49
Rousseau, J. J., 61, 62, 70
Russell, Bertrand, 101, 106, 107, 115, 122 f.

Salvation, 39
Santayana, George, 19, 23, 24 f., 105, chap. viii
Schopenhauer, Arthur, 81
Science and religion, conflict between, 19 ff.
Scientism, 120
"Secular," definition of, 15
Secularism, 16, 119
Silber, J. R., 77
Skepticism, 43 f., 109
Smith, Adam, 42, 60
Smith, J. E., 78
Socrates, 116
Spinoza, B. de, 19, 20, 21, 23, 25, chap. iii, 43, 45, 46, 75, 81, 93, 98, 116, 118
Substance, 37
Superman, 89, 122

Teleological argument; see Argument from design
Theology, 10 f.; ethical, 72; natural, 49; revealed, 49
Toleration, 13

Voltaire, 109

Wagner, Richard, 81, 85
Webb, C. C. J., 78
Wernam, A. G., 41
Will to power, 24, 79, 81 ff.
Wolfson, H. A., 41

Zoroaster, 88